MILLERS POINT

THE URBAN VILLAGE

SHIRLEY FITZGERALD &
CHRISTOPHER KEATING

HALSTEAD PRESS

SYDNEY MMIX

This edition published by Halstead Press
Unit 66, 89 Jones Street
Ultimo, New South Wales, 2007

and

Gorman House
Ainslie Avenue
Braddon, Australian Capital Territory, 2612

In association with the City of Sydney

© Copyright: Shirley Fitzgerald and Christopher Keating, 1991, 2009. Not to be copied whole or in part without authorisation. Typeset by Judi Rowe. Printed in Melbourne by Trojan Press.

First edition 1991, Hale and Iremonger Pty Limited

National Library cataloguing in publication entry

Fitzgerald, Shirley, 1949-
  Millers Point: the urban village / Shirley Fitzgerald & Christopher Keating.

  2nd ed.

  ISBN 9781920831653 (pbk.)

  Includes index.

  1. Millers Point (N.S.W.) – History.

  Keating, Christopher, 1960

  (Series: Sydney history series).

994.41

Millers Point, the urban village is a publication of the City of Sydney's History program

CONTENTS

Acknowledgements	4
Abbreviations, conversions	5
Introduction	7
1 Early Millers Point to 1850	9
2 From 1850 to 1900	48
3 From 1900 to 1939	73
4 From 1939 to the Present	109
Postscript	133
Sources of illustrations	139
Index	141

ACKNOWLEDGEMENTS

Millers Point: The Urban Village is the third in the Sydney City Council's series of studies of geographical areas of the city. Two earlier publications dealt with Chippendale and Surry Hills, while a fourth is a study of Ultimo and Pyrmont. These books form part of the Council's History Project undertaken as part of the Sesquicentenary celebrations of 1992. That year was marked by the publication of a major study of the Council and the city it presides over, while these smaller books, including *Millers Point* tell the social history of some of the distinctive areas which belong to it.

In preparing this book we acknowledge the ready assistance of many officers of the Council, the staff of the City Library, the Mitchell Library, the Maritime Service Board Library and the State Archives Office. The photographs and maps provided by these organisations are acknowledged in the list of illustrations at the end of the book. Several new maps were created by Dennis Robbie and Geoff Bradley of the City Engineers Department, while photographer Adrian Hall captured the delights of Millers Point in the 1990s.

When we first began to write this history of Millers Point there was a sense of being interlopers, of treading lately where may had been before. Interest in the area from a heritage point of view had resulted in many studies being commissioned by a variety of organisations. Because much of this work is in the form of unpublished reports to the Department of Housing and to the Maritime Services Board, we are indebted to the officers of these departments for their willingness to share this information with us. In particular, Tony Prescott of the Heritage Branch of the State Department of Environment and Planning gave generously of his detailed knowledge and understanding of Millers Point. He read and commented on the manuscript, as did Terry Kass, Janet Howse of the Council's Information Systems Department, Angela McGing of the Council's Archives Services and Robyn Conroy of the Council's Planning and Buildings Department, and Joyce Phillips of Millers Point. Jenny Wills typed the many drafts of the original edition with competence and skill. As with our previous books the manuscript was ably edited by Heather Cam.

The greatest pleasure in writing this book was gained from knowing that so many people were anxious to have their story told. In Millers Point it is difficult to distinguish between residents and local historians, for many are both. Conversation about the place comes easily in the houses and the pubs, and many people have shared with us their knowledge, their reminiscences and their photograph albums. Unpublished research material was made available by David Sheedy, Judy Wing and Patrick Callaghan. Oral and photographic material was given by many, but particular mention should be made of (in alphabetical order) Stephen Allen, Pam Anderson (Harry Jensen Centre), Shirley Ball, Tom Callaghan, Sharon Dodd-Gilhooly, Cecil Henry, Vera McDonald, Ted Musgrave, Joyce and Ray Phillips. In this book the voices of many other residents are also heard, through the use of interviews recorded by different researchers and journalists. The College of TAFE, Randwick, and the author have allowed us to use interviews from Trish FitzSimons' *'The Point's Changed a Terrible Lot'—Memories of The Rocks and Millers Point*. St Brigid's Church in Kent Street made available to us a series of interviews titled 'Point People'.

It became clear to us early on in this project that there was no end to the good will, interest and support of the many people who owe allegiance to Millers Point. Inevitably we have tapped only a portion of this local knowledge, and no doubt there have been many things we have left unwritten. They tell us in Millers Point that there is a book inside many of the local heads. We look forward to reading them.

2008

This is the third in the series of precinct studies undertaken in the 1990s which has been updated in 2008. As with the books on Chippendale and Surry Hills, the text has been lightly edited to correct inaccuracies or to take in new knowledge where appropriate, and a postscript has been added. The City's Archives staff updated the references to conform to current practice, and heritage planner Peter Woodley cast a critical eye over the postscript. Deborah Edward did additional picture research, and Paul Patterson provided new images where old ones had gone missing. Matthew Richardson and Alana Ayliffe at Halstead Press oversaw the editing and production, with design by Judi Rowe. The authors are, as ever, responsible for any shortcomings in the text.

Shirley Fitzgerald
Christopher Keating

ABBREVIATIONS

ADB	*Australian Dictionary of Biography*	NSWPD	*New South Wales Parliamentary Debates*
AGL	Australian Gas Light Company	NSWPP	*New South Wales Parliamentary Papers*
ALP	Australian Labor Party		
AR	Annual Report	NSW V&P	*New South Wales Votes and Proceedings*
CCS	Council of City of Sydney		
CHO	City Health Officer	PC	Proceedings of Council (Council of the City of Sydney)
CRS	Council Record Series		
GPO	Government Printing Office	PWD	Public Works Department
HRA	*Historical Records of Australia*	RC	Resolution of Council
JRAHS	*Journal of the Royal Australian Historical Society*	SC	Select Committee
		SCRA	Sydney Cove Redevelopment Authority
LA	Legislative Assembly		
LC	Legislative Council	SCSSHB	Sydney City and Suburban Sewage and Health Board
LMM	Lord Mayoral Minute		
ML SLNSW	Mitchell Library, State Library of New South Wales	SHT	Sydney Harbour Trust
		SMH	*Sydney Morning Herald*
ML SPF	Mitchell Library, small picture file	SRNSW	State Records of New South Wales
MSB	Maritime Services Board	TC	Town Clerk
MUA	Maritime Union of Australia	TCR	Town Clerk's Report
NSCA	City of Sydney Archives	WWF	Waterside Workers Federation
NSW	New South Wales		

CONVERSIONS

1 mile	=	1.61 km		100 ounces (oz)	=	2.83 kg
1 kilometre	=	0.62 mile		100 pounds (lb)	=	45.36 kg
1 foot (ft)	=	30.5 cm		1 ton	=	1.02 tonne
1 metre (m)	=	3.28 ft				

100 acres (ac)	=	40.5 hectares (ha)
10 gallons	=	45.5 litres (l)

Introduction

Millers Point in the 1990s was an area under close scrutiny as bureaucrats, heritage consultants and residents tried to define and identify the cultural and historical significance of this unique area of Sydney.

For much of its long history, however, The Point had been an out-of-the-way place: isolated initially by the stony terrain that divided it from The Rocks and, more lately, by the footing and ramparts of the Sydney Harbour Bridge. This isolation has helped preserve much of Millers Point. Emerging from the darkness at the western end of the Argyle Cut, the visitor steps into what appears to be a village, redolent of a Sydney that has elsewhere long since vanished under towers of concrete and glass. Many Sydneysiders have confused the area with The Rocks, but the people of Millers Point have fought to retain the identity of their community. And it is the survival of Millers Point as a residential neighbourhood that is the most significant difference between these two areas.

Millers Point has been home to a diverse array of people. For thousands of years prior to white settlement, Aboriginal tribes had speared fish from the deep waters off its rugged shores. More recently, convicts hewed stone from its quarries, while free men built windmills on its elevated ridges to grind grain. Later came the whalers, sealers, ships' captains and merchants who built wharves and rowdy taverns and then mansions and fine terraces perched high on the rocky knoll of Millers Point.

School fete, St Brigid's, 1990.

This bustling maritime enclave worked and slept according to the rhythms of the whaling and wool ships that anchored at The Point. Tales, both fanciful and true, were plentiful of the shanghai-ing and crimping of sailors, of smuggling and whoring and of the rough and sometimes exotic life typical of seaport communities. Later, this itinerant population of seamen and other 'birds of passage' was joined by a more settled congregation - waterfront labourers who filled the stone cottages and boarding houses of The Point, laboured hard by day at coal lumping or wool stowing, and swelled the thirsty crowds that gathered nightly at the multitude of local pubs.

From the 1870s, the economic base and, in turn, the class structure of the area became ever narrower as wool shipping and warehouses became pre-dominant in Millers Point. The skilled tradesmen and merchant princes moved out, but many of their fine mansions and elegant Victorian terraces remained. With the new century came the plague which led to the whole of Millers Point being annexed by the government, which has owned and administered it ever since. The Sydney Harbour Trust demolished many houses, refurbished some and built many others that still stand cheek by jowl with their nineteenth-century neighbours. For the rest of the century, the Trust, its successor the Maritime Services Board and, more recently, the Department of Housing have acted as state landlord. The stock of buildings has remained constant, with state ownership insulating Millers Point from the vagaries of urban property development and effectively 'freezing' the built environment as it was in the 1920s. The letting policies of the Trust and the MSB, which gave preference to local family members, helped to retain a close-knit and familiar community. Changes to this policy under the Department of Housing more recently sparked vigorous debate between residents and the government.

Several waves of urban redevelopment have swept through inner Sydney in recent decades, but at the beginning of the 1990s none had reached Millers Point. Its massive docks, its winding and elevated streets, its significant stock of housing and its stunning harbour views remained. All this made Millers Point unique and presented a complex challenge to governments and the urban power brokers who control Sydney's development. How that challenge was met is discussed in the Postscript to this book.

Watson Road leading from Argyle Street uphill to the Observatory Park demonstrates the steep topography of the area.

1

Early Millers Point to 1850

On 22 June 1826, John Leighton became exceedingly drunk. An ex-convict, he was 'a jovial though somewhat frugal man' and was known to all the locals as 'Jack the Miller'.[1] His house and three wooden windmills were perched high on a prominent, conical knoll of sandstone and scrub that projected into the waters of Port Jackson at the northwest corner of the peninsula dividing Sydney Cove from Cockle Bay, officially renamed Darling Harbour that year. The local Aborigines called the place Go-mo-ra. On that cold wintry evening Jack left his small house and clambered unsteadily up a ladder to one of the mills. From that vantage point, Jack could survey well the area that was to bear his name. The knoll of land he occupied was called Coodye, but in keeping with a general disregard for indigenous names, the colonials gave it the rather unimaginative title of Cockle Bay Point. It was more generally known as Jack the Millers Point. We know it today as Millers Point.

To the south Jack would have seen the headwaters of Cockle Bay, petering out into swamp and mudflat. Rising up on the east was the ridge now crowned by the Observatory, but then the site of the hexagonal battlements of Fort Phillip, a citadel built in 1804 to guard the town. Below the fort the land fell away in shelves and precipitous crags to the shores of Darling Harbour. A straggling footpath, later to be replaced by the less treacherous alignment of Kent Street, wound its way north towards Jack the Miller's Point along the rocky shoreline of Darling Harbour. This track skirted boulders, cliffs and numerous quarries and was impassable to all vehicles. Just to the north of those quarries the first street to penetrate the western side of the peninsula was named, not so surprisingly, Windmill Street. And stretching away to the northeast was the rock-strewn shoreline, later called Walsh Bay, that connected Millers Point with Dawes Point, known to the original residents as Tar-Ra. Turning north, Jack Leighton would have seen Goat Island (Memel) and beyond that the wooded bays of the North Shore. A more abstemious observer would have noted too the advancing tide of houses and maritime establishments that was gradually spilling over the ridge from The Rocks and creeping steadily northward along the eastern shore of Darling Harbour. But Jack the Miller was not very sober and far from observant—he fell from his ladder in a drunken haze and crashed to his death.[2]

In the early decades of white settlement at Sydney Cove, the Millers Point area was an inaccessible and far-flung backblock. Leighton had arrived as a convict in 1804 and by the time of his death in 1826, it was still only sparsely settled. However, to trace the evolution

---

1 Undated newspaper article, in 'Details of the Estate of John Leighton', ML SLNSW Doc 2964.
2 *Sydney Gazette*, 24 June 1826.

of the unique character of the area, we need to go back to the very beginnings of European occupation. In the late afternoon of 26 January 1788 the eleven ships of the First Fleet, by then eight wearying months out of Portsmouth, dropped anchor into the brilliant aquamarine of Sydney Cove. The ships bore a human cargo, a vanguard of 548 male and 188 female convicts, part of the 'excrementitious mass' of Britain's criminal classes.[3] Disappointment at the swamps and barren sands of Botany Bay and the disquieting encounter there with the French explorer La Perouse had spurred Captain Phillip on towards the more sylvan delights of Port Jackson, which he and Hunter had explored a few days earlier. Phillip wrote that this was 'the finest harbour in the world, in which a thousand sail of the line may ride with the most perfect security'. After examining its strange and primeval coves, he 'fixed on one that had the best spring of water, and in which ships can anchor so close to the shore that at very little expense quays may be made at which the largest ship may unload'.[4] Clearly, the new settlement was to be a maritime town, a dependant outpost reliant on shipping for its survival.

As the convicts and their gaolers mustered on deck, they beheld the strange features of War-ran (Sydney Cove), with Jubughalee (Bennelong Point) on the east and Tar-Ra (Dawes Point) on the west forming the valley through which the Tank Stream trickled into the tidal mudflats of the harbour. These landmarks were as yet unnamed by the white newcomers, but they had been familiar to the Aborigines for thousands of years. Here they had hunted and fished. They gathered shellfish from the mudflats around the shore, leaving large middens in what the Europeans would initially call Cockle Bay. They speared fish off the rocky promontories using small bark canoes. Within a few years, disease, most likely smallpox, would devastate the Aboriginal population.

All around the valley of the Tank Stream 'a majestic forest of Sydney red gums' flourished, and

> *huge myrtles with flesh of luminous rosiness. There were mimosas (speedily renamed 'wattles' because these small flowering trees were the first to be cut down and used in wattle-and-daub huts), and there were also turpentines, ironbark, blackbutt and the strange grass tree or blackboy, lifting its lance rimmed with downy light. In the humid recesses of the gullies grew orchids, mosses and ferns and a batallion of immensely tall cabbage-tree palms, which were cut down quick smart so that within a year not a palm remained.*[5]

Amidst great confusion the first groups stumbled ashore, each man stepping 'from the boat literally into a wood' below the long sandstone ledges and lintels of Tar-Ra, which would become Dawes Point.[6] Moving south along the western promontory of Sydney Cove these ledges rose up as formidable barriers, a jumbled series of cliffs, acclivities and jump-ups

---

3 Jeremy Bentham, quoted in Robert Hughes, *The Fatal Shore* (Pan Books, London, 1988), p 2.
4 Phillip to Sydney, 15 May 1788, *HRA*, Series 1, Vol 1, p 18.
5 Ruth Park, *The Companion Guide to Sydney* (Collins, Sydney, 1973), p 15.
6 David Collins, *An Account of the English Colony in New South Wales* (first published 1798, reprint A.H. & A.W. Reed, Sydney, 1975), Vol 1, p 5; Since 2001, the New South Wales Government has supported dual naming of places as part of the nation's reconciliation process. In 2002 the dual name of Dawes Point/Tar-Ra was gazetted.

Looking north towards Millers Point in the 1820s.

soon termed The Rocks. The peninsula was dominated by the high ground that Sydneysiders know today as Observatory Hill which still separates The Rocks from the Darling Harbour foreshore and from Millers Point. Coodye, as it was first known, was visible from the hill as a 20-metre high cone of land fringed by low rocks and, at low tide, by exposed sand and mud. Its sandstone base supported a thin and patchy soil and, like the other elevated ground around it, was 'scantily clad with a rufous fuzz, as though some prehistoric bushfire had flashed down the promontory and left it bare of all but wild flowers, grass trees and seastained scrub'.[7]

Access to this western side of the ridge and the point itself was not easy—the topography demanding either an ascent of The Rocks themselves or a precarious clambering over the rocky foreshore that stretched westward from Dawes Point. As we shall see later, the separateness of Millers Point from the rest of Sydney has been an enduring factor in the development of this unique area.[8] Although there were stretches of deep water relatively close to the rock-fringed shores of the point, the difficult terrain and the lack of easy access to the town deferred its early utilisation for maritime purposes, and the small size of the fledgling settlement meant that a discernible village centred around Millers Point would not appear until the 1830s.

---

7 Ruth Park, *The Companion Guide to Sydney*, p 14.
8 This separateness resulting from physical characteristics of the land may have parallels in the long time habitation patterns of Sydney's first owners. At the time of issuing the second edition of this book, scholarly work based on early European sources suggests that the people living around Go-mo-ra (Darling Harbour) may have formed a separate clan from the generally recognised Gadigal. Tentatively named the Gommerigal, this group has yet to be officially recognised. However, Arthur Phillip listed the Gomerrigal in 1790 as among 'other Tribes that live near us'. Early records locate these people at Long Cove, which is clearly the same place as Darling Harbour from the descriptions. As late as 1830, Absalom West recognised a 'Darling Harbour "tribe"'. The probable territory of the Gommerigal included land from Millers Point west to Blackwattle Bay: Keith Vincent Smith, 'Eora Clans: A History of Indigenous Social Organisation in Coastal Sydney, 1770–1890', Chapter 2.9, Gommerigal.tongara, pp 70–72, MA thesis, Macquarie University, Sydney, 2004.

Back in Sydney Cove the new arrivals struggled to establish a toe hold upon the 'savage coast' of New South Wales. According to Watkin Tench, an officer on the transport ship *Charlotte*:

> *Business now sat on every brow . . . In one place a party cutting down the woods; a second, setting up a blacksmith's forge; a third, dragging along a load of stores or provisions; here an officer pitching his marquee, with a detachment of troops parading on one side of him, and a cook's fire blazing up on the other.* [9]

But the business of setting up camp proved slow and was fraught with difficulties. Lack of tools and skilled artisans and the inadequacy of local timbers frustrated attempts at erecting decent houses and a desperate shortage of lime caused the mud-plastered walls of several huts to be washed to the ground during heavy rain. Most of the colonists sheltered in draughty canvas tents and the rows of tiny houses, so laboriously built, were little more than insubstantial humpies of wattle and mud. It took until early February to erect enough tents and huts to allow the last of the women convicts to be ferried ashore from the stinking holds of the transport ships.

By March 1788 the basic shape of the settlement had been established and Phillip's placement of buildings around the cove would have a lasting influence on the character and land use of the inner precincts of Sydney. The great social gulf that divided the town was the Tank Stream. On Bradley's map the patrician east is already well defined as separate from the plebeian west. The gentler slopes of the eastern promontory supported the government, the judiciary, the fledgling public service and the precious bounty of the Governor's garden. The residential character of the rocky western side was already well established, as was its role in the military and strategic support of the colony.

The western promontory of the cove in 1803.

9 Watkin Tench, *A Narrative of the Expedition to Botany Bay* (J. Debrett, London, 1789), p 60.

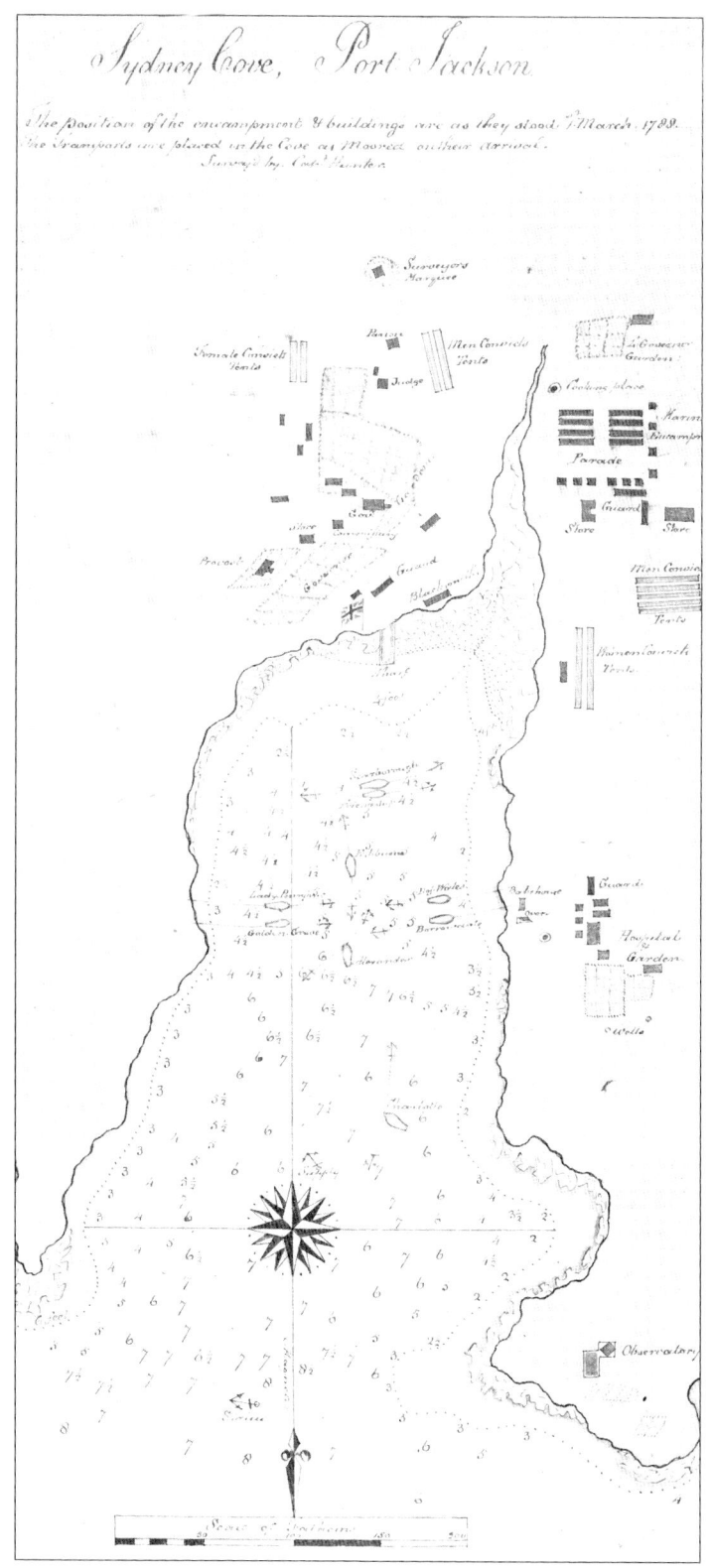

Bradley's map showing the layout of Sydney in 1788.

Significantly, the most detailed section of the map is Sydney Cove itself and the prominence afforded to the ships at anchor says much about British motives in colonising the place and notions of what its future should be. For the early colonists depending heavily on imports of manufactured goods and food, the ships meant survival, but they were also a sustaining symbolic link with Home. Physical and emotional sustenance came not from the wilderness that lay at their backs, but across vast tracts of ocean. Until the 1810s, they 'knew more about the Pacific Ocean and the southern seas than they did about the land which lay west of the Blue Mountains, only 100 kilometres or less from the town'.[10] Sydney was not founded for its own sake. It was not fashioned in its maker's image as an autonomous replication of England, but as a utilitarian depot to service the domestic requirements of Britain. In this the ships were vital—it was their cargoes, both into and out of Britain, that were the important thing, not the settlement of Sydney Town itself. The colony's reason for being was as a distant repository for the often unruly masses of excess labour generated by the industrialisation and urbanisation of Britain. In contemporary terms they were branded the 'criminal classes'. It was also to service British requirements as a supplier of wool and whaling products.

This outward-looking sense prevailed in Sydney until its motive force, transportation of convicts, ceased in 1840. By the 1850s Sydney had developed its own internal economies and self-supporting infrastructures: in short, it had developed its own reason for being.

Dawes Battery—more ceremonial than strategic.

---

10 Graeme Aplin and George Parsons, 'Maritime Trade: Shipping and the Early Colonial Economy', in Graeme Aplin (ed.) *A Difficult Infant: Sydney Before Macquarie* (NSW University Press, Kensington, 1988), p 148.

But in Millers Point, a maritime enclave servicing world markets in whale oil, seal skins and later in wool and gold, the outward-looking sense prevailed much longer and in no other community in Sydney would fortunes be more closely tied to foreign trade.

As Bradley's map reveals, the early settlement in Sydney Cove was more of a military encampment than a town. Throughout this early period the western peninsula of Sydney Cove continued to be used for strategic, scientific and various ancillary purposes. The parade ground and the marine barracks were centrally located on the western side. The hospital lay to the north of the convict dwellings with a bakehouse close to the shore and wells sunk nearby. The observatory occupying the end of the point was built by Lieutenant William Dawes, a man 'so much engaged with the stars that to mortal eyes he is not always visible'.[11] Dawes named the spot Point Maskelyne to honour the Astronomer Royal, but eventually his own name supplanted that of his mentor. A stone building replaced the temporary structure in mid-1788. When not gazing heavenwards, Dawes was in charge of the artillery of the colony and supervised the construction of Dawes Battery just next to the observatory.

This earthen redoubt was built in November 1788 and was armed with eight guns from the *Sirius*, but was replaced in 1791 by a small castellated Gothic fort which was positioned to 'annoy an enemy coming up the harbour'. Luckily, Dawes Battery was never put to such an onerous task. Royal birthday salutes were the limit of its fury, but even under such benign conditions one artillery officer lamented that the tiny fort 'falls to pieces when the guns are fired'.[12] It was eventually demolished to make way for the footings of the Harbour Bridge.

South of Dawes's observatory, the high ground we know today as Observatory Hill has had a variety of names. In July 1788 a flagstaff was erected there giving the area its initial name of Flagstaff Hill. The completion of the first government windmill on the site in February 1797 resulted in the alternative title, Windmill Hill. In March 1804 following the short-lived insurrection by Irish political prisoners at Castle Hill, Governor King order the building of a citadel to guard the town. Fort Phillip was begun soon after. Its battlements were designed to carry twenty four guns, but the fort was never finished and only six guns were installed. By mid-century it was demolished, the hexagonal foundations being used as the base of the present Observatory which was built on the site in 1858 and gave the locality the name it retains today. But such is the strength of the remembered past in Millers Point that older people today still sometimes refer to it as the Flagstaff, and recall that as children they used to go 'up the Flaggie' to play.

Just south of the Observatory a large military hospital was built in 1815, the building being renovated in 1849 and opened as Fort Street Model School in 1850. By then the new Victoria Barracks at Paddington had been completed and the huge barracks complex that had been built in 1818 near present-day Wynyard Station was demolished, its 15 acre site being cut up into building allotments.

---

11 Mrs Elizabeth Macarthur, quoted in Joan Lawrence, *Sydney From The Rocks* (Hale & Iremonger, Sydney, 1981), p 32.
12 J.H. Watson, *Old Sydney*, newspaper cuttings, p 94 (ML SLNSW).

A later sketch of one of the post mills on Jack the Miller's Point.

Perhaps the most visible feature of the western ridge of Sydney Cove was its windmills. Following the building of the windmill on Observatory Hill, Governor Hunter built another in about 1798, just to the south near present day Grosvenor Street. Prior to this, all grain was treated using either hand mills or walking mills. By 1812 Nathaniel Lucas had a wind-powered post mill just behind the battery at Dawes Point were he ground wheat at 15 pence per bushel. It is uncertain exactly when John Leighton began his milling operations. He did not gain his freedom until 1815, but he had already acquired several acres on Cockle Bay Point by 1814. The purchase was from the partnership of Lucas and Wall, but it is not known whether the sale included an operating mill.[13] By the 1820s, there were three wooden post mills on Millers Point, all apparently run by Jack the Miller. His original mill was near today's Bettington Street on the high ground just past Dalgety Terrace. According to John Rae, an early Town Clerk of Sydney, the second mill was built on land granted to Joseph Underwood in 1817 for 'the purpose of erecting a windmill thereon'. It was situated west of present day Merriman Street, but was demolished when a subsequent owner, John Jones, erected a terrace of three houses there just prior to 1842. The third windmill, in the Merriman Street area south of the second one, was still standing in the 1840s on land owned by a Mr Davis. The date of its final disappearance is uncertain.[14]

The windmills were notable landmarks in early Sydney. Alexander Harris sailed into Sydney in the 1820s and later recalled 'a waterside town scattered wide over upland and

---

13 J.P. McGuane, 'Sydney A Hundred Years Ago', in *Daily Telegraph*, 21 December 1912; Terry Kass, 'A Socio-Economic History of Millers Point' (NSW Dept. of Housing, 1987), p 21.
14 J. Skinner Prout and John Rae, *Sydney Illustrated* 1842–43 (Tyrrells Pty Ltd, Sydney, 1949), p 30; C.H. Bertie, *Old Sydney* (Angus & Robertson, Sydney, 1911), p 1; Town Surveyor's Report Book 1830–32, pp 74–75, SRNSW 9/2701.

lowland, and if it be a breezy day the merry rattling pace of its manifold windmills, here and there perched on the high points, is no unpleasing sight'.[15] Throughout this period the area became increasingly associated with Jack the Miller and several myths began to grow up around Leighton himself. One such legend purported that he was offered the whole of Millers Point as a land grant on the condition that he fence the narrow neck of land that gave access to its rocky heights, but he 'declined the expense and thus lost the land'.[16] His reputation for frugality perhaps stems from this unlikely tale.

Other industries were also underway in the area during these early years. On Dawes Point the colony's first slaughterhouse was in operation next to the battery, with Tom Cribb, the butcher, as overseer. Slaughterhouse Point was a common alias for the area. Lime for building purposes was in short supply and the abundant shellfish of Cockle Bay were burnt at lime kilns situated on Darling Harbour just below Fort Phillip. In the early years of settlement many of the shells came from local Aboriginal middens, but as these became depleted, supplies were shipped into Sydney from Brisbane Water, Pittwater and Botany Bay to be burnt at Millers Point. The now non-existent Lime Street (which ran south off Erskine Street, west of Sussex Street) commemorated another group of limeburners who operated further south in Darling Harbour from the 1830s and 1840s.[17]

The rocky nature of the terrain around Millers Point caused inconvenience to landowners. By 1823 Fort Phillip was 'encircled with stone quarries, and below these rises a line of streets and lanes that is frequently interrupted by large projecting masses of sandstone'.[18] Stone cutting had been underway in Kent Street North and at the rocky western end of Windmill Street since early in the century. This area was known locally as 'The Quarries' and provided much of the stone used to build early Sydney. By November 1830 there were six quarrying parties working there. George Hescot was granted permission by the Town Surveyor to work the old quarry in the intended line of Kent Street, an indulgence 'granted on account of his being blown up . . . in the employ of Government'. Toiling away just to the north of the one-eyed Mr Hescot was the widow, Lucy Bryant, who supported her large family by her labours. The intended prolongation of Argyle Street on the north side of Fort Phillip was being chipped at slowly by Mr Rocheford, with Joseph Lowe doing the same for the as-yet-unformed Fort Street.[19] The 'cutting down' of Millers Point for building lots, road formation and for port facilities was a process that would continue well into the twentieth century and would radically alter the shape of the village. In the mid-1820s changes of another variety were wrought by fuel-gathering children who chopped away indiscriminately at the bushes which clung to the slopes of Flagstaff Hill.[20]

---

15 Alexander Harris, *Settlers and Convicts: or Recollections of Sixteen Years Hard Labour in the Australian Backwoods* (first published London, 1847), (Melbourne University Press, Carlton, 1954), p 1.
16 Norman Selfe, 'Notes on Sydney Windmills . . .', *JRAHS*, Vol 1, Part 6 (1902–03), p 103. 17 Surveyor General's Sketch Books, Vol 4, pp 136 & 165, SRNSW X750A-X753; J.S.N. Wheeler, 'Old Millers Point, Sydney', *JRAHS*, Vol 48, Part 4 (August 1962), p 309.
18 J.T. Bigge, *Report of Commissioner of Inquiry on the State of Agriculture and Trade in the Colony of New South Wales*, 1823 (facs. edition, Libraries Board of South Australia, Adelaide, 1966), p 43.
19 Notice Book for Buildings on Town Allotments 1827–32, pp 124–28, SRNSW 9/2700.
20 J.A. Barry, *The City of Sydney: The Story of its Growth* (NSW Bookstall Co., Sydney, 1902), p 35.

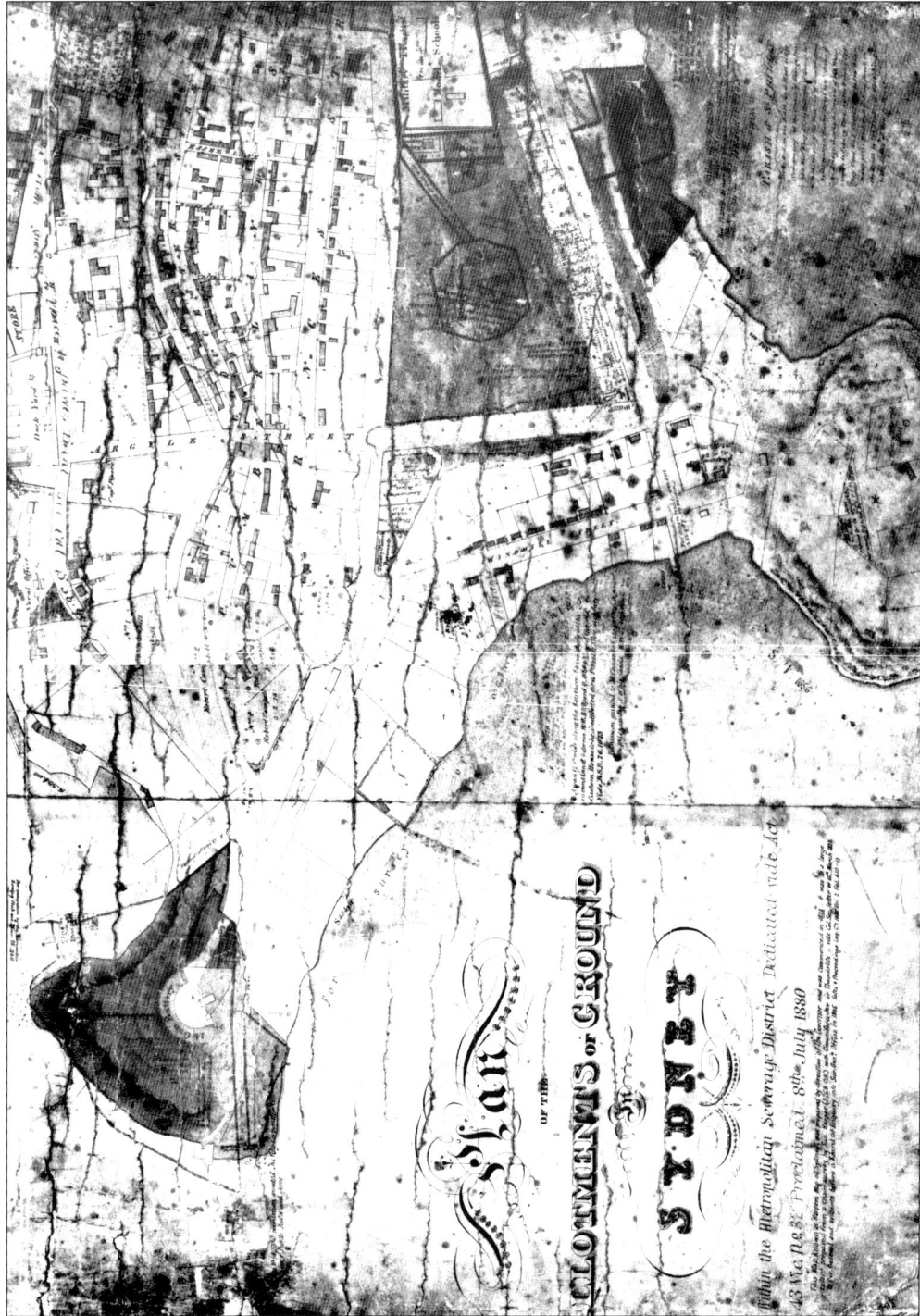

Harper's map was begun in 1823, with new buildings and road alignments being added later. By the mid-1820s most of the land on the point and in Walsh Bay had been alienated.

By the time of Jack Leighton's death in 1826, Millers Point was still relatively undeveloped. Harper's map, begun by 1825, gives some idea of the pattern of early settlement. However, many of the features of this map were added much later than 1825, so, while it is not historically accurate for that year, it does help us to place the early houses, roads and tracks in relation to a familiar streetscape. The most notable post-1825 additions are the alignments of Kent and Argyle streets. Neither existed in Millers Point in 1825 and access to the area for vehicles was via Dawes Point and Lower Fort Street. The track that skirted the Darling Harbour foreshore west of the future Kent Street was for hardy pedestrians only. Just past The Quarries it veered east to join Lower Fort Street, with another branch winding along the rocky heights of Millers Point itself. Windmill Street in 1825 did not extend beyond the intended alignment of Kent Street. Although most of the land had been alienated by then, only seven houses were scattered across the point. Several houses fronted Windmill Street (although some of these may be later additions) and, directly behind them, four more faced the foot track that led from Darling Harbour to Lower Fort Street and approximated the future line of Argyle Place.

But change was close at hand for Millers Point. By the early 1800s the western shore of Sydney Cove contained a growing concentration of maritime, shipbuilding and warehousing facilities. South of Dawes Point lay the wharf and stores of pioneer merchant Robert Campbell, the colony's first private wharf owner. Nearby were the Naval Dockyard and the large Commissariat Stores built in 1812. By this stage the original government wharves in Sydney Cove were small and dilapidated with certain cargoes having to be thrown overboard and swum ashore. In 1813 Governor Macquarie commissioned the building of a 'spacious and commodious quay', the King's Wharf, to replace them.[21] Shipbuilding was underway in the cove at James Underwood's yard from as early as 1789 and at the Naval Dockyard from 1796. As population increased the residential occupation

Sydney in the 1820s. On the right are Dawes Point, with Fort Phillip above it, and the windmills of Millers Point behind.

---

21 F. Matthews, 'The Development of Wharfage: Sydney Harbour 1788–1825', *Port of Sydney*, January 1947, p 72.

of The Rocks area intensified. By the 1820s the streets were narrow and straggling and the houses, described by Cunningham as 'rows of neat white cottages', but by James Tucker as 'no better . . . than huts', faced in all directions.[22] Alexander Harris recalled that The Rocks was the low-life section of town, frequented by felons, prostitutes, drunken sailors and ruffians. It was a place of crowded, narrow alleys, foul grog shops and seedy dosshouses.

In 1823 Commissioner J.T. Bigge stated that there was 'little space now left upon the sides and shore of Sydney Cove for the construction of commercial buildings' and Cunningham reported soon after that on the other side of the ridge there were 'various tasteful white cottages' facing Darling Harbour which attested to the fact that

> the 'vulgar Rocks' is eagerly essaying to throw off the plebeian slough in which it has long been enveloped, and to take its station among the more genteel quarters of the town. Mercantile wharfs and warehouses . . . are fast rising here too . . . Darling Harbour bids fair soon to rival Sydney Cove in bustle and importance.[23]

By the late 1820s then the focus of residential, commercial and maritime activity was expanding to include the western side of the peninsula. The wharves and warehouses mentioned by Cunningham were as yet still located in the south of Darling Harbour near the Market Wharf, but in the next few decades such industries would encroach on Millers Point from the south and also from Walsh Bay to the north-east.

He also prophesied that, unlike the seedy and vulgar Rocks area, the western slopes and Millers Point would be industrious and respectable. This social distinction between the two localities would prove to be a more enduring factor than the separateness caused by the topography. Even today the Millers Point area is erroneously included by many Sydneysiders as part of The Rocks, an assumption which still brings vehement protests from the residents of The Point. It was in the 1830s then that the village of Millers Point started to take shape as maritime and commercial concerns began to be located away from the congestion of Sydney Cove. Many of the wharf owners, ships' captains and associated merchants chose to settle there too, as did the artisans and labourers they employed.

The early history of land ownership in Millers Point is very complex. We know from maps that most of the Windmill Street area, Walsh Bay and The Point itself was in private ownership by the 1820s, but how these owners acquired their property is less certain. Many received grants of land, but poor administration and lack of documentation meant that, in fact, many pieces of land 'were simply occupied by a system closely akin to squatting, [and] once such parcels of land had been sold to another person, the government found it difficult legally or morally to divest such later owners of their land'.[24] By 1823 Commissioner Bigge stated that 80 per cent of houses in Sydney were permissive occupancies.[25] In 1831 the Town Surveyor, Ambrose Hallen, reported that John Clarke had

---

22 P. Cunningham, *Two Years in New South Wales* (Henry Colburn, London, 1827), second edition, Vol 1, p 38; James Tucker, *Ralph Rashleigh* (Angus & Robertson, Sydney, 1975), p 69.
23 J.T. Bigge, *State of Agriculture and Trade*, p 43; P. Cunningham, Two Years in New South Wales, Vol 1, pp 85–86.
24 Terry Kass, 'A Socio-Economic History of Millers Point', p 3.
25 J.T. Bigge, *State of Agriculture and Trade*, p 42.

fenced in an allotment of the government reserve on the south side of Windmill Street where the Hero of Waterloo Hotel now stands. When his right to do so was challenged, Clarke produced a legal transfer from Jack Leighton's son and heir, David, who had bought it from Patrick Marmount, who, in turn, claimed to have received the land from Governor Macquarie as compensation for another of his allotments which was resumed for the new Military Hospital built in 1815. Clarke pleaded that he had come free to the colony with a large family and had saved, 'with the greatest frugality and industry', the considerable sum he had paid for the land.[26] It took until April 1841 for a grant to be formalised for this land under a special commission set up to deal with such claims on land.

Other claims were based on alleged promises of land made by long-departed Governors. In 1830, an old man named James Townsend, whose wife had been the nurse to Governor Macquarie's wife, claimed that Macquarie himself had promised him land on the waterfront in Kent Street fifteen years ago as 'a recompense for his having constantly conveyed the Constables by water to Lane Cove when in pursuit of bushrangers'.[27] Not surprisingly, by the mid-1830s, the system of administering and recording land grants and the ownership and transfer of land was greatly confused. From the late 1830s, a Commissioner of Claims issued Crown grants for most of Millers Point, but as the occupation and sale of land in the area had been under way for years prior to this, the grantees were mostly not the original occupiers of the property. Around the waterfront areas of Walsh Bay and Millers Point the lots granted were relatively large and represent prior purchases by a growing group of colonial merchants seeking waterside facilities to enter the booming import/export trade.[28] Sufficient land was no longer available in Sydney Cove and from the mid-1820s these merchants steadily acquired tracts of land in Millers Point.

One of the earliest was William Walker, who built the first wharf near the Dawes Point end of Walsh Bay in the 1820s. His mercantile career was typical of many of the traders who helped build early Millers Point. Like most of them he began his colonial wanderings as an agent for an English mercantile firm, but settled in Sydney in March 1820. He used his wharf and warehouse near Dawes Point to move into coastal shipping (bringing timber, coal and produce to Sydney) and the high risk, but highly profitable, whaling industry. During the late 1820s he was importing Saxon merino ewes to stock the vast tracts of pastoral land he had been granted and by the late thirties the well-established family company of Walker Bros & Co. was a major exporter of wool to London.[29] He was joined in Walsh Bay by other prominent merchants like John Lamb, Timothy Gordon Pittman and the partnership of Alexander Berry and Edward Wollstonecraft. By 1831 much of the north side of the point itself had been bought up by the publican, William Long and his partner, the wealthy brewer, James Wright, who had acquired two large blocks from T.G.

---

26 Town Surveyor's Report Book 1828–32, pp 73–74, SRNSW 9/2701; Commissioner of Claims Draft Reports 1841, No 637, SRNSW 2/7647.
27 Notice Book for Buildings on Town Allotments 1827–32, p 141, SRNSW 9/2700.
28 Terry Kass, 'Socio-Economic History of Millers Point', p 4.
29 Vivienne Parsons, 'Walker, William (1787–1854)' *ADB*, Vol 2, 1967, p 566.

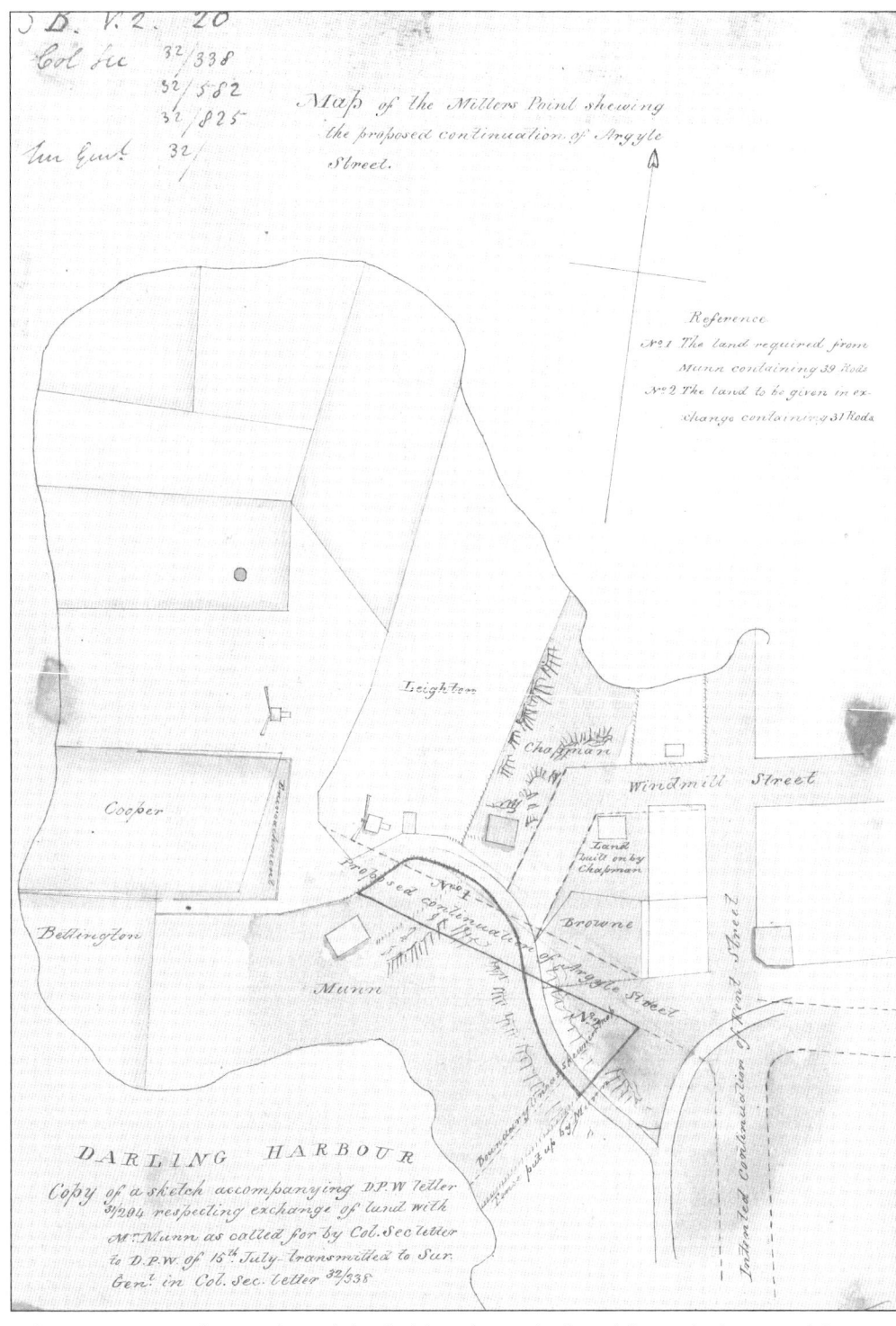

Millers Point in 1831, showing the early landholders, the windmills and the tracks that served the area.

Pittman on the northern tip of The Point, plus the next door allotment—the one originally occupied by Jack Leighton. They soon built a bearing-down wharf for the repair of ships and began filling the harbour foreshore to accommodate wharves and warehouses for 'the convenience, benefit and advantage of the shipping and mercantile interests of the colony.' This property was later acquired by Joseph and Henry Moore in 1837.[30]

John Irving and William Henry Chapman were both boat builders who had been residents of Millers Point since the early 1820s. Chapman owned the waterside block on the north side of the narrow neck of the point. This land was immediately east of Leighton's block and backed onto the elbow at the western end of Windmill Street. During the early thirties he ran a wharf and boatshed there until the property was subdivided and sold in 1837. Irving operated on just over one acre of waterside land on the north-east corner of Kent and Windmill streets. The merchant, pastoralist and wharf owner, J.B. Bettington, occupied land on the south-west corner of the point. By 1832 his wharf and stores were busy with colonial whalers and timber vessels. The now vanished Munn Street commemorated the early Millers Point shipbuilder, James Munn, who owned more than two acres of hilly waterfront land next to Bettington, fronting the southern indentation of Darling Harbour. After buying out his other neighbour, Arthur Martin, Munn operated a floating dry dock (130 feet long and 50 feet wide) which in 1831 lay on the shallow, tidal mudflats of Darling Harbour.

Further south on the Darling Harbour foreshore large tracts were taken up by A.B. Spark, Matthew Bryce, John Terry Hughes and, below the government reserve, by Thomas Agar and Elizabeth Jenkins. Inland from these large mercantile blocks were smaller residential allotments facing Windmill Street and the as-yet-unformed Argyle Place, many of which were snapped up during the buoyant economy of the 1830s by prominent Sydney land buyers F.W. Unwin, J.T. Hughes and John Hosking.[31]

The timing of the development of commercial and mercantile life in early Millers Point reflects well the status afforded to New South Wales by its British masters. In the 1820s, Commissioner J.T. Bigge lamented the fact that industry and trade would continue to languish so long as the colony was 'occupied and treated as a receptacle for convicts'. Security fears saw the introduction of restrictive port and tonnage duties and 'absurd regulations' that deterred ships from entering Port Jackson. At the same time, the powerful British East India Company's monopoly on trade in the Indian and Pacific oceans resulted in duties being imposed on colonial wool and whale oil in Britain, restricting local ship owners. These attempts to maintain New South Wales as a convict dump and nothing more were resisted locally and not surprisingly the most prominent agitators against the reintroduction of transportation were the merchant ship owners. It was not until the 'convict incubus' had been thrown off that the merchants of Millers Point 'flocked in and established great houses' for trade. This progressive change of attitude in the thirties was signalled by a relaxation of duties and restrictions, with the last of the monopolies on the

---

30 Terry Kass, 'Socio-Economic History of Millers Point', p 4; Town Surveyor's Report Book 1830–32, pp 74–78.
31 Nancy Gray, 'Bettington, James Brindley (1796–1857), *ADB*, Vol 3, pp 158–59; NSCA CRS 26/155/13 (Map, T.A. Dibbs to TC, 30 December 1878).

China tea trade being lifted in 1834, and culminated in the abolition of transportation to New South Wales in 1840.[32]

In the restrictive trading environment of the 1820s, the development of wharf activity in Walsh Bay, Millers Point and north Darling Harbour was piecemeal. The following two decades, however, saw a period of increasing population and despite a severe depression in the early forties, there was a widening demand for staple goods. Colonial vessels had long used the waters off Millers Point as deep water anchorages, using small lighters to move goods and crew between ship and shore. None of the new wharves were deep water berths, however, and long stages had to be run out from the wharf itself to the ships. It was the boom in coastal shipping and increasing colonial involvement in the lucrative whaling trade and in the consignment of wool to London in the 1830s and 1840s that brought a vigorous phase of wharf-building activity to Millers Point. In these decades the coastal trade was still an important activity in Millers Point. J.B. Bettington's neighbour, John Bingle, was the first to establish regular services to and from Newcastle and from 1822 carried coal, cedar and merchandise, whilst much of the Shoalhaven produce was landed by Berry and Wollstonecraft at Duke's Wharf or at Jones's Wharf on the north-eastern side of The Point.[33] North coast cedar and New Zealand kauri pines for re-export were landed at the Lumber Wharf in Walsh Bay in the early 1840s and oyster shells at Kennedy's Limeburners Wharf near Jones's Wharf. About the same time, the Australian Agricultural Company which had multifarious interests in the Newcastle and Port Stephens areas had a wharf and coal depot on the western shoreline.[34]

Eber Bunker, the 'father of Australian whaling'.

William Walker's neighbour in Walsh Bay, John Lamb, was born in 1790, the son of an East India Company captain. He arrived in Sydney in 1829 and with his cousin, Walter Buchanan, set up as a merchant, wool broker and shipping agent. With a speculative zeal typical of these early merchant princes, Lamb proclaimed that although he intended to remain only ten years in the colony, he would triple his starting capital. In the thirties he was running the schooner *Darling* in the coastal trade, with the brig *Amity* plying the Indian Ocean for sugar from Mauritius. He appears to have avoided the whaling trade but, as we shall see later, his firm, Lamb Parbury & Co., became one of the dominant forces in the wool trade. Bott's Wharf, Pittman's Wharf and Shepherd and Alger's Wharf were other early arrivals in Walsh Bay.[35] The merchant firm of Aspinall Brown & Co. took over Berry

---

32 J.T. Bigge, *State of Agriculture and Trade*, pp 56–61; P. Cunningham, *Two Years in New South Wales*, Vol 2, pp 66–67; *Sydney Mail*, 24 October 1896.
33 Nancy Gray, 'Bringle, John (1796–1882)', *ADB*, Vol 1, p 102; *Evening News*, 30 May 1905.
34 J. Skinner Prout and John Rae, *Sydney Illustrated*, p 31.
35 *ADB*, Vol 2, pp 72–73; Mary Salmon, 'Towns Wharf', *Evening News*, 29 May 1911.

and Wollstonecraft's Millers Point wharves in the 1830s. The small colonial fleet that 'dodged along the coast', bringing food and produce to Sydney from the expanding river valley settlements, would increasingly congregate in the south of Darling Harbour near the Market Wharf (Market Street), but the unmistakable stench of the black-hulled whaling fleet would linger for decades around Millers Point.

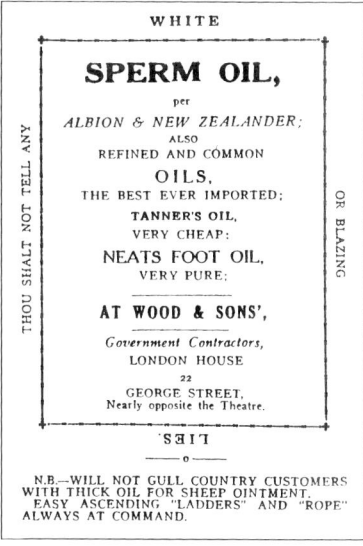

Whaling and sealing were the colony's first major export industries. It was not until 1835 that wool overtook the products of the 'whale fisheries' (whale oil, whalebone and seal skins) as the major export from New South Wales. An early mayor of Sydney, George Thornton, remembered that the first contract to light the town was fulfilled using sperm whale oil. In June 1827 he recalled the lamplighters being followed by a crowd of boys singing satirical songs as the streets were lit. The lamps were a great advance, but their dullness sufficed only to 'make the darkness visible'.[36]

As early as 1791 Captain Thomas Melville left Sydney in the storeship *Britannia* in company with the Third Fleet convict transport *William & Ann*, commanded by Eber Bunker, and killed seven sperm whales, the first taken in Australian waters. An 'able and expert Seaman', Bunker has been called the 'father of Australian whaling'. The designation Bunker's Hill, which for many years was applied to the northern end of The Rocks, commemorated his early exploits.[37] By 1802 there were seven whalers operating from Sydney and by 1804 they were joined by eleven ships engaged in the equally gruesome Bass Strait sealing industry which landed 100,000 skins in Sydney in the six years after 1800.

English and Americans were soon flocking to the southern fisheries and, despite a monopoly held by the East India Company which banned colonial vessels from direct trade with Britain, the local fleet continued to expand. In about 1827 at their wharf in Walsh Bay, William Walker and his partner Richard Jones owned the first locally based vessels, which included the barques *Wolf* and *Lynx* and the 250 ton *Mary*. By 1835 there were seventeen whalers in the Sydney fleet, plus scores of British, European and American whalers.[38] The catches and potential profits were phenomenal. In 1831 just under thirty ships docked at Sydney, having killed over 2,900 black and sperm whales and nearly five thousand seals. The largest ship was the 527 ton *Hashemy* which employed thirty seven men. A less ambitious venture was undertaken by two hardy sealers who returned to port in January 1831 with 200 seal skins worth one pound each after an epic fifteen month voyage in a tiny three ton boat named *Mary*.[39] During the 1840s it was said in Sydney that 'every north-east

---

36 *Sydney Mail*, 24 October 1896.
37 The Macquarie Book of Events (Macquarie Library, Macquarie University, 1988), pp 75, 170; ADB, Vol, p 178.
38 *The Macquarie Book of Events*, pp 169–70; Mary Salmon, 'Towns Wharf', *Evening News*, 25 May 1911.
39 'Return of Fisheries for the Year 1831', in SRNSW 4/7267.

Left: Henry Moore—his storehouses, built by William Long in 1835, still stand at Millers Point.
Right: Robert Towns—after success in the whaling and South Sea trades he moved into land and pastoral speculation. Townsville is named after him.

wind blows a whaler' and by then Millers Point was very much the hub for the deep sea ships whose owners dabbled not only in whaling but in wool consignment and in the Pacific Island trade.[40] In this decade the major wharves in Millers Point were owned by Henry Moore who bought Long's Wharf in 1837 and the irrepressible speculator, Captain Robert Towns, who took over Jones's Wharf next door in 1844. At these and other wharves:

> *The ships gave to the locality the scent of the sea. Whaling and the South Sea Island trade were in their hey-day. In the stores lining the waterfront a strange motley array of products appeared. Sugar, dark brown in colour, known as 'custard sugar', packed in big bamboo baskets; seal skins; salt from Cape Verde; sandalwood; wheat; sperm and black oil and whalebone spoke of other lands. In the streets wandered crews of many ships—Europeans, Americans, Colonials, tattooed New Zealanders, Chinese and South Sea Island boys . . .*[41]

In the 1820s the Islanders contributed to the exotic colour of Sydney:

> *In the streets of Sydney . . . may often be seen groups of natives from various of the numerous South Sea Islands, with which we trade, in all their eccentricities of*

---

40 *SMH*, 12 March 1909.
41 A.W. Morton, *History of the Garrison Church: Holy Trinity, Sydney*, (Anglican Diocese of Sydney, 1940, reprinted 1977), p 3.

costume. A considerable portion of Otaheitians and New Zealanders are employed as sailors in the vessels that frequent our port' and in the evening, as you stroll along the picturesque shores of our harbour, you may be often melted with the wild melody of an Otaheitian love-song from one ship, and have your blood frozen by the horrific whoop of a New Zealand wardance from another, the shrill piercing notes of which thrill through you with a sensation as if these cannibals were pouncing with brandished war-clubs upon you to glut their appetites with the tempting picknick fate had thus placed in their way.[42]

Captain Joseph Moore left England in 1812 bound for the southern 'sperm fishery'. After several seasons in the trade he acquired a share in the firm of Jones & Walker and settled in Sydney in 1820. His son Henry also joined the firm and in November 1837 they bought the wharf and stores belonging to William Long on the northern tip of Millers Point. Joseph died in 1857 and Henry Moore took over. For over sixty years Moore's Wharf was one of the busiest on The Point and it was not until the early 1900s that Moore's Road was renamed Dalgety Road. Moore's Bond Store was built in 1835 by William Long using rock cut from the site, and is a fine example of early commercial architecture. It still stands today, but was relocated in 1978 to the site of Town's Wharf.[43]

Robert Towns was born in 1794 in Northumberland. Although he had little formal education, he gained command of a ship in the Mediterranean trade at the age of nineteen after studying navigation at night. In 1827 he arrived in Sydney with a general cargo and within five years was bringing out bounty immigrants and merchandise in his own ship, *The Brothers*, making a trip almost every year. By 1833 he secured his position amongst the colonial power structure by marrying Sophia, the half sister of W.C. Wentworth. He settled in Sydney in 1843 as a mercantile agent and local representative for Richard Brooks & Co. of London. In 1844 he wrote to London that 'I consider myself a "lifer", here, as I am buying a wharf.' That year he bought Jones's Wharf which was next to Moore's Wharf on the northern foreshore of Millers Point. He lived at Victoria Terrace and various other mansions, which overlooked his wharf, and for the next twenty years he worked a twelve hour day, seven days a week 'as regular as the platipus'. Robert Towns was blunt and abrupt in his manner and gained a reputation as 'the incarnation of the puritan virtues of thrift, sobriety, industry and perseverance'.[44]

Towns was also the archetypal merchant speculator. Like those of his competitors Moore and Walker, much of his early profits came from whaling, but he speculated in almost every commodity the Pacific region had to offer. From the mid-forties he was sending horses, known as 'walers', to Calcutta; sandalwood, turtle shell and bêche-de-mer to Canton; merchandise and provisions to New Caledonia; wool and whale oil to London. On their return to Sydney, his ships brought sugar and rope from Manila; rice from India;

---

42 P. Cunningham, *Two Years in New South Wales*, 1827, Vol 1, p 58.
43 David Sheedy Pty Ltd, 'A Study of the History of Bligh House, 43 Lower Fort Street' (typescript, December 1990), p 3; J.H. Watson, 'Australian Mariners of the Past', *The Scottish Australian*, March 1918, pp 6190–94.
44 D. Shineberg, 'Towns, Robert (1794–1873), *ADB*, Vol 6, pp 294–96; *Evening News*, 30 May 1905.

wheat from Valparaiso and salt from Cape Verde, with each arrival carefully timed, or delayed on purpose, to take advantage of periodic shortages in the local market. By 1851, Towns was running thirteen ships and his wharf at Millers Point was 'a veritable South Island township' where dark-skinned sailors toiled amidst a jumble of casks, boxes, whaling tackle and merchandise.[45]

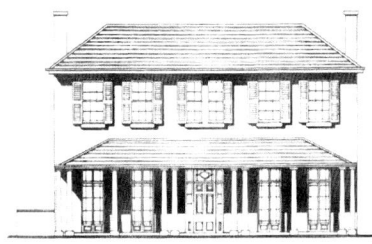

Clyde Bank, 43 Lower Fort Street.

During the thirties and forties maritime activity at Millers Point became increasingly export oriented. Bigger warehouses and wharves were erected by Moore, Towns and Lamb to ship the ever-increasing tonnage of wool which was displacing whale oil as the predominant cargo on the Millers Point wharves. It was in these decades that the village of Millers Point emerged, as merchants, sailors, artisans and labourers moved in to work within the growing maritime and mercantile infrastructure of the area.

By 1839 Maclehose observed that Sydney had begun 'to assume the appearance of a regular well built town'. Millers Point was now the site of various wharves which, despite steep and inconvenient land access, still had spacious storehouses. Kent Street extended all the way to Argyle Street via 'a deep cut . . . in the west side of the hill on which Fort Phillip stands', but it was still inaccessible to carriages beyond The Quarries. The houses in Kent Street progressed steadily northwards during these years as level sites became available. Most were 'of the humble order of wooden

The Garrison Church (Holy Trinity) and the Argyle Cut.

---

45 W.J. Dakin, *Whalemen Adventurers in Southern Waters* (Angus & Robertson, Sydney, 1977), p 117; *Evening News*, 29 May 1911.

huts'. A long-enduring exception was the pair of cottages built in the early 1820s by stonemason Thomas Glover in Kent Street and known for years as 'The Ark'. They are reputed to be the first semi-detached cottages built in Sydney and still stand today, perched above the level of the street next to the imported relic, Richmond Villa.[46]

Windmill Street was 'the high-street of shipping interests in that direction, overlooking, as it did the chief wharves where the whaling vessels did most congregate'. As late as 1839 it was still only partly built on, although it commanded one of 'the finest prospects in Sydney'. However, the increasing concentration of maritime activities in Walsh Bay in the 1840s saw the street fill up with ship's chandlers, sailmakers, carpenters and block and tackle makers, as well as those indicators of itinerant maritime communities—the boarding house, the brothel and the pub.

Later sketch of Clyde Street or Scotch Row.

In Lower Fort Street, however, Maclehose reported that 'a number of respectable dwelling houses have lately been erected on the north side of the street, having a fine appearance from their uniformity of build, and are mostly occupied by opulent persons.'[47] The refined air of this wealthy locality was established early on by Clyde Bank, which was home to a succession of Sydney's mercantile elite, including Joseph Moore, John Terry Hughes and Robert Campbell junior. The house was built in 1824 for Robert Crawford, the principal clerk to the Colonial Secretary. Joseph Moore acquired the house in 1835, around the time he and his son Henry purchased Long and Wright's wharf. The house has been variously named Bligh House, Holbeck and St. Elmo. It was used as a boarding house for many decades of the twentieth century, then by the Australian College of General Practitioners, and as a private museum. Another fine example of early quality housing still stands at 37 Lower Fort Street which dates from the late thirties. Just along the road the Australian American Association presently occupies a 'crisp and elegant pair of late Georgian townhouses' at 39–41 Lower Fort Street. They are the only surviving example of John Verge's small scale domestic designs and were built in 1836 for speculative purposes. Maclehose claimed that this part of Millers Point was 'as a whole . . . probably one of the best neighbourhoods in Sydney'.[48] Further quality residences were added in the succeeding decades and stamped this area as a secure upper middle class enclave.

---

46 J. Maclehose, *Picture of Sydney and Stranger's Guide in New South Wales* (J. Maclehose, Sydney, 1839), pp 62–63; Howard Tanner & Assocs., 'Millers Point: Statement of Significance and Related Policy Considerations' (NSW Dept. of Housing, 1987), p 15.
47 'Old Sydney by Old Chum', ML SLNSW Newspaper Cuttings, Vol 8, p 144; J. Maclehose, *Stranger's Guide*, p 78.
48 David Sheedy Pty Ltd, 'A Study of the History of Bligh House', p 2; Royal Australian Institute of Architects (NSW), *Photographic Guide to the Architecture of Sydney: No 1 City Centre* (pamphlet, 2nd edition); J. Maclehose, *Stranger's Guide*, p 78.

A view from Observatory Hill. The eccentric design of Albion House dominates this rather stylised picture. The Lord Nelson Hotel is on the right.

On the heights of The Point itself 'a very considerable population' had assembled by the late 1830s. The original foot track that led west off Kent Street was now honoured by the rather too grand title of Millers Point Road (later Millers Road). Various stony tracks plunged south and west from this road, giving a somewhat precipitous access to the waterfront. Clinging grimly to this southern face of The Point was a scattering of small cottages that overlooked Bettington's Wharf and James Munn's shipyard. Most were occupied by labourers and artisans. The first street to the west of Kent Street was Clyde Street, which rang with the broad accents of its Glasgow-born occupants. Mostly stonemasons, these men and their families were brought to the colony in 1831 by the religious firebrand Rev. J.D. Lang, partly to dilute what he saw as the dangerous influence of the idle, drunken Irish. The street was quickly renamed 'Scotch Row'. Beyond the hollow that led down to the shipyard was another range of cottages, located close to where Munn and Unwin streets would later be formed.[49] By 1834 the land facing Wentworth Street just west of Clyde Street was subdivided and sold off as building allotments.

The area west of Kent Street and bounded by Millers Road on the south and Argyle Street on the north was also cut up for house blocks. David Leighton had been selling off small parcels of land on the top of Millers Point since the late twenties. The piecemeal way in which this was done greatly complicated government attempts in the 1840s to establish who had legal title to their land. There were no large scale subdivisions of land in Millers Point. Rather there was, from the thirties, a gradual but fragmentary process whereby the

---

49 J. Maclehose, *Stranger's Guide*, p 77; J. Skinner Prout and John Rae, *Sydney Illustrated*, p 30.

larger grants were broken up into house-sized allotments. As a result, house building was similarly diffuse and intermittent.[50]

By the late thirties other small artisans' cottages were scattered across The Point, in Kent Street and along Windmill Street. Here gathered the labourers and tradesmen drawn to the shipping and warehousing activities around the foreshore. And on The Point itself were built several large and opulent houses that rivalled those in Lower Fort Street, and established the area as 'a very high-toned neighbourhood' in which 'some of the first people resided'.[51] Albion House was 'a fantastical looking building' in the Italianate style built in about 1826 for William Davies on the north side of the roadway to Bettington's Wharf. In 1832 it was advertised to let as a 'magnificent marine villa'. In the thirties the daughters of the local gentry were there learning the finer points of etiquette at Mrs Brown's ladies' seminary and by 1843 Mr Johnson ran the house as a boarding establishment.[52]

The prime residences in Millers Point were clustered around what is now Clyne Reserve, a small elevated park at the northern end of Merriman Street. Today a sheer cliff drops from the western side of this street to the low level port facilities that face Darling Harbour near the monolithic Maritime Services Board tower. This reclamation by the MSB during the 1970s saw nearly half of the original area of The Point disappear. To venture west of Clyne Reserve today would involve a fatal and final step into mid-air, but in the 1830s it brought the 'merchant princes' of Millers Point home to their mansions. At the end of Merriman Street a road, later called Dibbs Street, ran west to Spencer Lodge, the most famous of the area's houses. Over the road lay Darley House, and to the north were Moorecliff and Victoria Cottage which were reached by way of Victoria Terrace, another street of quality houses that is known today as Dalgety Terrace.

These houses were a tangible statement of the prominence of mercantile gentry in early Millers Point. From their shady verandahs they could gaze down upon their ships, their wharves and warehouses, and upon the humbler abodes of the labourers, artisans and sailors who sustained their speculative endeavours. Spencer Lodge was a twelve room brick and shingle colonial townhouse with every convenience and a garden complete with 'lawns, rosaries and plantations of flowering shrubs'.[53] It was built in 1835 for a Mr Edwards who lived in London and the first occupant was that exemplar of his class, the wealthy merchant John Lamb. The late thirties were good times for the Moore family. Soon after the purchase of Long's Wharf in 1837, Henry Moore built Moorecliff next to Victoria Cottage. A succession of prominent citizens, including Robert Towns and his partner, the future Premier, Alexander Stuart, occupied Moorecliff. Benjamin Darley, who was Robert Towns's brother-in-law and sometime partner, was ensconced at Darley House. A procession of colonial gentry resided in the row of houses that made up Victoria Terrace which overlooked Towns's Wharf from the early 1840s. Of all these dwellings the grand terrace houses now at 7–13 Dalgety Terrace are the only survivors.

---

50 Terry Kass, 'Socio-Economic History of Millers Point', p 8.
51 'Old Sydney by Old Chum', *Truth*, 24 November 1907.
52 J. Skinner Prout and John Rae, *Sydney Illustrated*, p 30; J.S.N. Wheeler, 'Old Millers Point, Sydney', p 307.
53 *Sunday Times*, 8 September 1901; NSCA CRS 17/6/2 (Gipps Ward Assessment Book, 1845).

Demographically, Millers Point from this period was a well rounded village, containing the wealthy owners and employers, a wide variety of skilled tradesmen and a large complement of labourers. A large proportion from each of these categories lived and worked in the village itself, making it a highly self sufficient and even insular community. It was not like Surry Hills, for example, a dormitory suburb for the wider economy of Sydney, nor was it a manufacturing provider like the Sussex Street area. It existed to service overseas trade and was, in many respects, a village apart from the rest of Sydney.

There was a wide variety of work available in Millers Point, but most jobs were connected with ships or with the cargoes they carried. As early as 1832 Wright and Long were advertising for 'forty stout labourers' to work their wharf at Millers Point, for which they would be paid six shillings a week, plus rations of flour, beef, sugar, tea and soap.[54] Work was intermittent, often back breaking and continued until the loading or unloading was completed, with shifts of sixteen hours being commonplace. Until late in the century the organisation of wharf labouring was very haphazard. In this early period, the casual waterside labourers objected strongly to the use of seamen and convicts to handle cargoes, but effective opposition to the shipowners was still a long way off.

Wool shipping was an increasing employer of local labour. In 1838 there were twelve hand-operated wool presses in Walsh Bay, as well as one hydraulic press owned by Aspinall Brown & Co. Other locals were employed in offloading of incoming bales from drays, and in rolling the pressed bales up the long stages to the ship's hold where loading was done by stevedores. This entire process was extremely labour intensive and only four cranes were in operation by 1838. This was a boom year on the waterfront and many of the Walsh Bay occupants carried on more than one line of business. George Talbot of Windmill Street was a ship and anchor smith, but also operated six lever wool presses. Local labourers and artisans could seek work from the shipsmith, John McMillan, at Josiah West's mast and block factory or at Moore's cooperage. A wide variety of skilled tradesmen worked in local boat-building yards run by John Redgrave, Joseph Faris and Andrew Summerbell.[55] Shipbuilding had been underway at Munn's yard since the 1820s. In about 1844 Lawrence Corcoran took it over and within a few years the yard, under its foreman and subsequent owner, John Cuthbert, was turning out substantial ships like the 148 ton brig *Wild Irish Girl*, built in 1848 and sold to a local shipper for £2,500.[56] Throughout the forties, maritime support services continued to concentrate in Millers Point and drew increasing numbers of labourers, tradesmen and, of course, sailors to the area. Quarriers and stonemasons were still well represented.

During the 1830s quarrying of the sandstone outcrops around Millers Point had continued, but by 1839 Argyle Street was still divided by 'a precipice of considerable height', into which some rough steps had been cut to allow pedestrian access between Millers Point and The Rocks.[57] Plans to drive a cutting through the rocks had been devised as early as

---

54 C.H. Bertie, *Old Sydney*, p 4.
55 Magistrates Return of Mills, Manufactories, etc. 1831–42, SRNSW 4/7267.
56 *Sun*, 3 January 1911.
57 J. Maclehose, *Stranger's Guide*, p 79.

1832. With the support of local merchant houses such as Aspinall Brown & Co., Millers Point landowner F.W. Unwin proposed an Argyle Street Company be formed to make the cut, using convict labour. This and other schemes languished for a decade until the government made a start on it in 1843, using 'working parties of chain-ganged convicts in yellow and grey [who] came down each morning from the Hyde Park Barracks . . . to do their patient picking' under the tyrannical eye of overseer Timothy Lane.[58] Not all Millers Point residents wanted to be linked so directly with the rest of Sydney, fearing that the proposed cut would introduce into the area an undesirable class of people. The interests of the mercantile gentry prevailed, however, and the scheme was eventually completed as part of the formation of the Semi-Circular Quay with spoils from the Argyle Cut used to reclaim much of the foreshore of Sydney Cove in the late forties. From about 1845, labourers from the newly formed Sydney Council completed the work and by about 1859 three wooden overhead bridges spanned the gap in Princes, Cumberland and Gloucester streets.[59]

The City Council was formed in 1842 and during its first few precarious decades was beseiged by petitions and letters complaining about the poor state of the city's drainage, sewerage, roads and the often non-existent water supply and lighting. The Council was hampered by a lack of funds and faced with a huge backlog in the provision of basic services. And even when a water or sewerage main was laid, it had no power to compel landlords to connect their houses to it. Progress was thus slow and halting.

In the 1830s access to supply of water was very much a matter of either personal endeavour or financial resourcefulness. Those without their own wells had to make daily trips to various public wells or were forced to buy it by the bucketful from water carters. There is evidence of a well near Merriman Street and a 'well for public use' was installed by William Chapman near his wharf in Windmill Street which he sold in 1837.[60] Much of the area's water was brought up in casks from the outlet to Busby's Bore in Hyde Park. It was sold by water carts at a penny a bucket and 'if you did not take water from the man in winter, he would not sell you any in summer [and] if you had a cask full of rain water he would not serve you. He did very well out of his monopoly of the water supply'.[61] The City Council laid on piped water to many of the streets in Millers Point in the 1840s, but only a few of the wealthier residents had their houses connected to the mains. The reluctance of tight-wad landlords meant that the majority had to endure the bullying of the water-carters or line up at the municipal fountains or pumps that tapped into the mains. As late as 1852 shipping in Millers Point was still being supplied by water carts like the Phoenix Water Tank owned by John Stubbs of Windmill Street.[62]

Sewerage services were much slower in arriving. By mid-century the only sewer main in Millers Point ran along a section of Windmill Street.

---

58 Terry Kass, 'Socio-Economic History of Millers Point', p 6; Isadore Brodsky, *The Streets of Sydney* (Old Sydney Free Press, Sydney, 1962), pp 20–21; Letter to brother Carroll, 21 October 1946, p. 41ff. (ML SLNSW MSS A3175).
59 J.A. Barry, *The City of Sydney*, p 39.
60 Hughes, Trueman and Ludlow, 'Wells and Underground Tanks' (Heritage Council of NSW, Sydney, 1984), p 56.
61 Eliza Walker, 'Old Sydney in the Forties', *JRAHS*, Vol 16 (1930), p 313.
62 NSCA CRS 26/7/10.

The Australian Gas Light Company was formed in 1837 and built its works on Darling Harbour just to the south of Millers Point. The first gas lights were turned on in 1841, but by 1849 there were only six public lights in The Point. Publicans were then required to erect lamps in front of their premises so Millers Point, with its abundance of pubs, was perhaps better lit than official figures suggest. In 1842 over sixty four per cent of the gas lamps in Sydney were hotel lights.[63] The elevated site of Millers Point made it one of the healthiest quarters of the city, but its topography caused many problems with drainage and road formation. With the beleaguered Council running for cover, many of the local worthies resorted to self help. In 1848 George Talbot paved and kerbed 200 feet of the roadway in Victoria Terrace and built a stone parapet wall to prevent the road being washed by heavy rain down 'the deep precipice between Victoria Terrace and the road to Moore's Wharf'. Despite his opinion that the wall was not securely built, the City Surveyor suggested that Council pitch in with a surface drain to carry away any water. The three dimensional nature of The Point's terrain would cause problems for years to come. Since Talbot's efforts many similar attempts were made to shore up this precipice below Victoria Terrace, now Dalgety Terrace. As late as 1990 this cliff face was still rebelling against its confinement, when tons of earth and rock and iron railing crashed from its height to Dalgety Road below.

In 1846 a petition signed by 'the most influential Mercantile Firms in this City' drew the Town Clerk's attention to the 'dilapidated state of the roads leading from Kent and Fort streets to Millers Point'. These roads were rocky, steep and unformed, causing a great inconvenience to the public and 'considerable injury . . .. to the valuable Wharves' that depended on them for access. According to the City Surveyor the surface drainage in Clyde Street was 'so insufficient as to cause a great nuisance' and somewhat reluctantly Council agreed to kerb and gutter both sides from Millers Road 'to the Rock near the water's edge'.[64]

Robert Towns was a vituperative critic of the newly appointed city fathers. In 1849 he accused the City Surveyor of wilful damage and of 'obstinate inattention' to his requests for a stone facing at the water's edge at the end of Kent Street to stop the accumulation of silt and rubbish at his wharf. He claimed that the water had shoaled two and a half feet in three years, but the fact that the construction of this improvement might well be his own responsibility did not seem to have deterred the irascible Mr Towns. A more down-to-earth complaint came from former Town Clerk C.H. Chambers who pointed out that 'the shores of Darling Harbour are lined with dead dogs and that the putrescent state of the atmosphere thereby occasioned is positively pestilential'.[65]

By mid-century Sydney was still a fairly rough and ready town. The municipal authorities had struggled to alleviate the worst of the environmental and residential disasters, but lack of funds, inexperienced administration and a hostile government hampered their efforts to make a dent in the enormous backlog in the provision of

---

63 NSCA CRS 21/7, Report No 24; *Sun*, 6 October 1910.
64 NSCA CRS 21/7, Report No 18; NSCA CRS 26/3/57; NSCA CRS 21/7, Report No 9.
65 NSCA CRS 26/4/230; NSCA CRS 26/8/58.

This photograph, taken in 1900, shows the simple mid-century cottages of Clyde Street.

services. According to visiting commentators, the drains were all on the surface, the sewerage was 'shamefully bad' and the paving and lighting were 'a disgrace to the city and its corporation'. All this was true of Millers Point, with one observer claiming that its streets were 'bad and dirty'.[66] In most regards, however, the area was far better off than many parts of Sydney. It was steeper and rockier than other localities, but it is this elevation that also made it drier and healthier than the sunless alleyways of The Rocks and Sussex Street, the swamps and sand drifts of Surry Hills, or the polluted watercourses of Chippendale, Redfern and Ultimo.

The fortunes of this largely self-contained maritime village expanded steadily in the thirties. Expansion continued erratically in the volatile economy of the forties. During the dramatic depression of the early forties, the speculative mercantile firms were hit hard. Henry Moore was forced to sell off much of the land he had accumulated, mostly on the North Shore, to stay in business. But gradually confidence and opportunities for employment returned to Millers Point. The population increased steadily as artisans moved in to take up jobs in the trades associated with shipping. Since much of the

---

66 G.C. Mundy, *Our Antipodes* (Richard Bentley, London, 1852), Vol 1, p 41; R. Elwes, *A Sketcher's Tour Round the World* (Hurst & Blackett, London, 1854), p 282.

labouring work on the wharves, in warehouses and in shipbuilding was casual and intermittent, many labourers came to live in Millers Point to be close to the sources of employment. This was a period of steady residential infilling with small stone and brick cottages packing ever closer along the rough streets.

For the purpose of striking a city rate the Council completed its first comprehensive assessment of city property in 1845. In the mind of the assessor, Millers Point was still a scattered and somewhat ill-defined village. Clyde and Wentworth streets were by then sufficiently established to receive a separate entry, but Bettington, Munn and Unwin are described merely as a group of seven properties at the 'rear of Kent and Clyde Streets'. Moore's Road, Victoria Terrace and Crown Road (later Merriman Street) are identified in the assessment book only as 'Millers Point'. In the south, Gas Street, Jenkins Street and Crescent Street (later part of Grosvenor Street) clustered around the Gas Company's works. There were 299 houses in Millers Point by 1845. Kent Street and Windmill Street were the most populous with fifty and thirty four houses respectively, while fifty nine houses were located in the three streets lumped together as 'Millers Point'.[67]

Sandstone, much of it quarried locally, was used to build over half of the houses. Brick was a significant building material only in wealthier streets such as Upper and Lower Fort streets and on The Point itself. Over ninety six per cent of the houses were shingled and only the well-heeled residents of Victoria Terrace made use of slate roofing. Similar class distinctions are reflected in the size of the houses. Most of the humbler abodes on the south side of The Point had between two and four rooms. By today's standards these simple cottages seem tiny, but in 1845 they were accepted as quite adequate dwellings, with almost seventy two per cent of Millers Point houses having four rooms or fewer.

In the newly formed Wentworth Street which ran down towards Corcoran's shipyard, Mary Farrell lived in a one room wood and shingle cottage owned by local landlord and publican, George Paton. In 1845 she paid the lowest level of rent in Millers Point (£10 a year or three shillings and ten pence a week) for a house in bad repair and described as having 'no outhouses'. This does not refer to any failure on the part of the landlord to supply a toilet, but indicates the lack of a proper kitchen which in those days were built detached from the house due to the fire hazard. In the more rarefied atmosphere of Crown Road, the wealthy wool shipper, John Lamb, luxuriated amidst 'every convenience and garden' in the twelve room mansion, Spencer Lodge, for which he outlayed £175 per year in rent. Between these two extremes was the typical two or four room stone and shingle cottage which could be rented for £20–£30 per annum. Thomas Glover's houses which still stand today in Kent Street exemplify the 'average' house in early Millers Point.

Only sixteen per cent of all the houses in the area were occupied by the owner in 1845, the rest being rented out. This is a remarkably high proportion of rental housing. In most studies of early Sydney rental housing is used as an indicator of the relative poverty of an area. As we have seen, however, Millers Point was not a poor and predominantly working class area. It did contain a majority of labourers and semi-skilled tradesmen, but strongly

---

67 Gipps Ward Assessment Book, 1845.

represented were the skilled artisans and small business operators; and, as well as the mercantile gentry, there was an influential group of moneyed professionals based in Victoria Terrace, Crown Road and in Upper and Lower Fort streets. An area where twenty eight per cent of the housing stock had five or more rooms was far from being a slum. The high proportion of rental housing was not an index of poverty, but reflects certain socio-economic and demographic factors that made the community unique in Sydney.

Most occupations in the area were connected with shipping. The village thus had a narrow and highly specialised economic base which produced a community characterised by a highly mobile workforce, a low level of family formation and a large population of itinerant 'blow-ins' from overseas ships. In short, the types of jobs carried on in Millers Point meant that for many it made little economic sense to buy a house. The labourers on the wharves and in the numerous small workshops were casually employed. Wharf labourers in particular were at times without work for weeks. The intermittent and seasonal nature of their work denied them the long term financial stability that buying a house requires. With no guarantee of work, they were highly mobile and were at times forced to move to other ports to keep in work. Many of the merchants had a rather tenuous link to Sydney. As agents for London firms they retained strong links with England. As speculators in a volatile world market they held no particular allegiance to Sydney and their arrival here was often motivated not by a fervent longing to settle in Australia, but by an often temporary speculative advantage that made Sydney more profitable than Calcutta, the Cape or any other imperial trading depot where, under different market conditions, they may just as easily have settled. Significantly, Robert Towns's decision to become a 'lifer' in Sydney was not prompted by his earlier marriage into local society or by any plan to acquire a house, but by the purchase of Jones's Wharf in the depression of the 1840s. The fluctuations possible in the fortunes of these merchants militated against a long term attachment to any of the frontier outposts between which they migrated. And business sense would have told them that money tied up in housing would bring a far more lucrative return if invested in a ship instead. Although Towns did settle down in Millers Point he, like many of his competitors, rented for years after his arrival. In 1845 nearly all of the 'marine villas' and up-market terraces in Millers Point were rented out.

Seamen on the whaling and wool ships were even less likely to purchase a house. In 1846 an American writer observed that the 'true sailormen have always been a class apart' and that the whaling fleets of the world were 'a place of refuge for the distressed and persecuted, a school for the dissipated [and] an asylum for the needy'. He added that he would 'sooner be in the penitentiary any time'.[68] This is a rather bleak and negative view of the type of person that crewed the whalers, wool ships and merchantmen of the world. The common sailors were indeed a class apart and, although they were not all misfits or alcoholics or criminal absconders, these traits were certainly more noticeable among the colonial tars than among their shore-bound cousins. Whatever the degree of truth

---

68 W.J. Dakin, *Whalemen Adventurers in Southern Waters*, pp 69–71.

The first St Philips Anglican Church.

contained in these observations they suggest, as does the fact that such men could be away for years on end, that sailors were not of the marrying kind. Clearly it was easier and cheaper to rent a cottage or stay in a boarding house when in port. These single men contributed to a generally low level of family formation in the Millers Point community in the nineteenth century. It was a community of itinerant residents in which males, many of them single, greatly outnumbered females. All these interconnected factors discouraged home buying in Millers Point.

In addition to this, the village played host to a sizeable population of foreign sailors, resting and revelling between trips. Certainly they were unlikely to be in the market for a house, yet they still required accommodation. Although Millers Point had its share of seedy dosshouses, the more infamous of these establishments—hotels like the Black Dog and the Sheer Hulk, which also catered to the alcoholic and sexual proclivities of the sailors—were located in The Rocks. Of course, the same types of services and accommodation could be readily procured in Millers Point, but so could the more homely and up-market comforts of the area's many boarding houses. They are still a notable feature of Millers Point today.

In many ways Millers Point was a self-sustaining village from the 1840s. The locals lived, worked, shopped and socialised close to home. Many of them had little cause to venture beyond the inner precincts of the city and knew more about the dockside areas of Newcastle, Brisbane and other ports than they did about the sprawling city that lay beyond the familiar confines of Millers Point.[69] And the churches, schools, shops and pubs built in the area during the 1830s and 1840s meant that they had even less reason to leave the area.

---

69 Personal Communication with Shirley Ball, January 1991.

St Brigid's church and school in Kent Street is the oldest Catholic building in Australia. In 1833 Governor Bourke approved the site and building plans for 'a Roman Catholic School House, to be occasionally used as a Chapel'. Construction began in 1834 using stone which was 'close at hand', and the simple one storey church was completed in April 1835. Four years later Edward Hawkely was teaching seventy six boys, and beyond a folding partition the forty five girls were in the charge of Mary O'Brien. For years the church and school were known as St Bridget's and the new spelling was not adopted until 1930.[70] The foundation stone of St Patrick's, the parish church nearby in The Rocks, was not laid until 1840. The land for this fine Gothic church was donated by William Davis, an Irish political convict who was known in Sydney as 'the Wexford Pikeman' for his part in the Irish rebellions of 1798. It still stands today in Grosvenor Street.[71]

The first Anglican church of any substance to serve the people of Sydney was St Philips, located near St Patrick's on what was called 'Church Hill'. Its clock tower fell down twice before it was completed and it was finally consecrated in 1810. It was an 'afflicting building like a brick marquee' and was quickly labelled 'the ugliest church in Christendom'.[72] By 1840 it was too small and the foundation stone of Holy Trinity, which stands today at the corner of Argyle and Lower Fort streets, was laid in June of that year. The original church was designed by Henry Ginn and built by Edward Flood, but was intended only as a temporary structure. From the outset the trustees agreed that as there were 'many sailors and other persons residing in the neighbourhood of Dawes Point, at least one-fourth of the sittings should be free'. The effect that this display of largesse had on the hard-bitten seafaring population is not recorded, however, and it was the military

Fort Street School.

---

70 'St Brigid's Church and School' (pamphlet, nd).
71 Eliza Walker, 'Old Sydney in the Forties', p 303; 'Old Sydney by Old Chum', *Truth*, 27 October 1907.
72 Joan Lawrence, *Sydney From The Rocks* (Hale & Iremonger, Sydney, 1988), p 28; Ruth Park, *The Companion Guide to Sydney*, p 55.

Redcoats at Dawes Battery, 1842.

garrison at Dawes Battery, not the sailors, who became closely associated with the church. Until the 1880s, the redcoats of the 50th Queen's Own Regiment marched up Lower Fort Street from the artillery barracks to attend morning prayer at what is still known as the 'Garrison Church'. Military parades on a grand scale were a feature of the church and numerous regimental banners still hang along its walls. By the 1830s, a parish school was operating in Princes Street, but it was later moved to what is now the parish hall next door to Holy Trinity.[73]

The parochial schools attached to these churches provided the only education for many of the local children until the opening of Fort Street Model School for Girls and Boys in 1850. Originally the building was a Military Hospital designed by Lieutenant John Watts and built in 1815, but after the military left it was enlarged sometime in 1849 by renowned architect Mortimer Lewis. The encasement of the old building was in the Victorian Mannerist style, and it is currently considered to be a fine example of its type, although an earlier assessment was that it was 'probably Lewis's worst architectural effort'. The 'aggressively solid old pile' drew its first teachers from the Irish National School service. For the next fifty years Fort Street was a leading elementary school and teacher training centre.[74] For those families who could afford it, there were several private academies in the area. Deportment and etiquette were a big part of the curriculum at Mrs Brown's school for ladies at Albion House and at Mrs Perrier's in Lower Fort Street. For 30 guineas a year, young ladies could obtain board and tuition at Mrs Boatwright's seminary across the ridge on Bunker's Hill; and up and coming gentlemen could endure the disciplinary rigours of Mr McRobert's private classes on Church Hill.

It is perhaps true that few of the educational benefits of the area trickled down to the

---

73 A.W. Morton, *History of the Garrison Church*, pp 4–8.
74 Royal Australian Institute of Architects (NSW), *Photographic Guide to the Architecture of Sydney*; Douglas Williams, 'The Beginnings of Australia', *The Australian Magazine*, 1 April 1908.

children of the sailors and labourers of Millers Point. A more frequented part of the social infrastructure was, no doubt, the seemingly endless array of local pubs. The history of the early hotels in Millers Point is very confusing. At various times, there were three pubs called the 'Whalers Arms' (or 'Old Whalers Arms') in the village, plus another in Gloucester Street in The Rocks. One of the earliest stood near the corner of Windmill and Lower Fort streets and was run by Joseph Faris in 1831. By 1842 Faris was running the Young Princess Inn which was next door to his former hotel, which by then had become known as the 'Old Whalers Arms'. By the 1850s the Young Princess had been renamed the 'Whalers Arms'. Another Whalers Arms stood on the northwest corner of Argyle and Windmill streets, this being 'the first hotel to be encountered by whalers when they came up the slope of Moore's Road from their ships at Towns's Wharf'. Other early pubs were the Shipwright's Arms (1831), the Steam Packet (1835) and the Blacksmiths Arms (1836) all in Windmill Street and the Quarryman's Arms (late 1830s) in Kent Street. The Royal Oak Hotel dated from 1837 and stood in Millers Road which curved west from Kent Street to meet Argyle Street. By 1847 the licensee, John Pomroy Bond, was advertising that he had 'good accommodation for Captains of vessels and others'. Not far away in Clyde Street was the Rainbow Inn (1837) which was sold in 1843 as a 'house of call for tradesmen and mechanics living at Millers Point'.[75] Boatbuilders and tradesmen were prominent among the early licensees of Millers Point. Among them were Joseph Faris, John Redgrave, John McMillan and George Paton.

The most famous pubs in present day Millers Point are two survivors from this early period, the Lord Nelson and the Hero of Waterloo. The older of these is the Lord Nelson built by the former plasterer, William Wells, during the 1830s. Wells obtained a licence to

The Victoria Arms, the Royal Oak and the Lord Nelson clustered around the end of Argyle Street. The tall building in the centre is Merriman Terrace on Crown Road, now Merriman Street.

---

75 J.S.N. Wheeler, 'Old Millers Point', pp 310–19.

run the building as a hotel in June 1842 and the pub still operates today, having the oldest liquor licence in New South Wales. During the forties the hotel was faced across Kent Street by the Napoleon Inn which stood as 'a sort of national opposition to the Lord Nelson'.

George Paton was a stonemason who had worked on the building of the Garrison Church and became a substantial property owner in Millers Point. In 1843 he built the Hero of Waterloo Hotel on the corner of Lower Fort and Windmill streets using sandstone brought up from the Argyle Cut. It is a powerful though austere building and retains many of its original features, including its massive timber framework. It was first licensed in 1845 and today is one of the favourite watering holes in Millers Point. This hotel was the source of many Millers Point stories of concealed trapdoors, rum smuggling and the shanghaiing of sailors. These colourful yarns persist to this day. Tunnels can still be seen in the cellars of the Lord Nelson and the Hero.[76]

To be a publican in Millers Point was a fairly sure means of obtaining financial security. In the fifties G.C. Mundy observed that the day labourers of Sydney were 'notoriously idle, drunken and dissolute' and in their drinking propensities the dockside labourers and itinerant sailors of The Point were certainly no slouches. But Mundy's subsequent comment that they chose to work only four days out of seven and for the rest of the week squandered their gains 'in drink and riot' reveals his ignorance of the social effects of irregular and unregulated hours and casual 'pick up' employment. After a sixteen-hour shift loading wool or an eight month whaling voyage, a 'cleansing ale' was welcome no matter what time of the day or week it happened to be.[77]

Certainly the corner hotel was central to the social lives of many Millers Point residents, but the area did provide a range of more moderate pastimes. J.B. Martin recalled that 'the lower tastes' of many Sydneysiders were catered for at Morris's cockpit, at sparring bouts, dog fights and at certain 'free and easy clubs'. Up until the 1830s, swimming was common in Darling Harbour and William Govett remembered girls as young as eight 'plunging fearlessly off into very deep water'. Daylight bathing was eventually banned by the government, but it was the pollution of the harbour that would ultimately prove a greater deterrent to such sports. Fishing was common around the small jetties and Sir James Fairfax recalled that his first such attempt, near Towns's Wharf, was rewarded by the capture of a bullock's skull.[78] Those with more refined tastes were obliged to go beyond Millers Point for entertainment. There were concerts at the School of Arts or a trip to the Royal Victoria Theatre in Pitt Street to hear the warblings of Theodosia Yates or to see Mr Geoghegan's play *The Hibernian Father*. Fiddlers or a military band could be hired for private functions and piano lessons could be arranged with Mr Stubbs, the auctioneer.[79] On public holidays like Anniversary Day or St Patrick's Day, there were skiff races on the

---

76 Ibid, pp 313, 317; *Daily Telegraph*, 29 April 1985; *SMH*, 11 April 1989.
77 G.C. Mundy, *Our Antipodes*, Vol 1, pp 50–51.
78 J.B. Martin, *Reminiscences* (A.J. Doust, Camden, 1884), p 41; William Romaine Govett, *Sketches of New South Wales*, (Gaston Renard, Melbourne, 1977), p 68; Frank Walker, 'Millers Point and Vicinity', *MSB Officers Journal*, February 1938, p 28.
79 M. Barnard Eldershaw, *A House is Built* (Lloyd O'Neil, 1977), p 155; J.B. Martin, *Reminiscences*, pp 40–41.

Harbour or whaleboat races from Dawes Battery to Shark Island and back.[80]

G.C. Mundy said that Sydney was generally a peaceable town, but recalled that the wildest disturbances were 'to be traced to the garrison and to the shipping'. Now and then, he said, a group of grenadiers would clear a taproom or 'a knot of able seamen [might] be seen battling the watch, or experimenting in horsemanship, to the danger of all landlubbers'.[81] In October 1841 the British man o' war HMS *Favorite* berthed at Millers Point. Fortified by a day of drinking, the sailors began a wild brawl outside the Royal Victoria Theatre with a contingent of the infamous Cabbage Tree Mob, a renowned larrikin push that gained its name from the distinctive 'cabbage tree' hats they wore. After two of their number were arrested, the sailors stormed the Cumberland Street watch-house using a jib boom as a battering ram. A night of rioting followed. The St James and the Central watch houses were threatened and the growing crowd was only stopped after troops fired a volley of warning shots, upon which the police and the soldiers 'fell promiscuously on all and sundry without regard to age or sex'.[82] During the 1843 Legislative Council election contest between Wentworth, Bland and the local shipping identity, Captain Daniel O'Connell, John Jones and a group of whalers stormed the polling both on Flagstaff Hill and, armed with harpoons and staves, assailed Captain O'Connell's detractors and drove them 'over the rocks on Flagstaff Hill to Argyle Street'. Throughout the night the 'excited populace stormed and fought and threatened' and the polling had to be postponed.[83]

The larrikin pushes were a more consistent threat to law and order. The Cabbage Tree Mob were 'an unruly set of young fellows, native born generally' who dressed in 'a suit of fustian or colonial tweed' and were distinguished by their low-crowned cabbage palm hats. In the 1840s and 1850s, Bristley's Mob claimed the Wynyard Barracks area as their own. Another band of roisterers was The Forties who 'smuggled and drank and swore, and paid no man reverance'. The Rocks Push claimed to be the oldest and most powerful of all the larrikin gangs, having been formed in about 1841 by an ex-convict stonemason named Slick.[84] The golden age of the pushes, however, was yet to come. In the eighties and nineties the Millers Point Push was fully matured and wholly antagonistic toward its bully boy counterparts from The Rocks.

Stories of smuggling in the Millers Point and Darling Harbour areas are common. Evasion of market dues and custom duties was somewhat of a tradition in early Sydney, and the caves and gullies of the Hawkesbury River concealed illegal grog stills. Humphrey McKeon remembered a typical episode from his youth:

> *One dark night my father heard a vessel come alongside the wharf and unload a quantity of kegs, and in a very short time a good number were taken off, presumably to the cellars of some neighbouring inn. Next morning there appeared the Customs*

---

80 J.A. Barry, *The City of Sydney*, p 20.
81 G.C. Mundy, *Our Antipodes*, Vol 1, p 56.
82 *Sunday Telegraph*, 8 February 1981.
83 Frank Walker, 'Millers Point and Vicinity', p 29; Roderick Quinn, *The Old 'Rocks': A Sketch of their History* (NSW GP, Sydney, 1902), pp 3–4.
84 G.C. Mundy, *Our Antipodes*, Vol 1, p 53; Isadore Brodsky, *The Heart of The Rocks of Old Sydney* (Old Sydney Free Press, Sydney, 1965), p 87.

Ships at anchor off the wharves at Millers Point. Henry Moore's storehouses are visible on the extreme right.

> *House officer who, coming on the wharf, began to poke about among the barrels of beef and pork, and to look with suspicion among the bags of potatoes. They had all come from the Hawkesbury and so had considerable quantities of locally made rum, for stills abounded in the caves and inaccessible recesses of that river. It's too long ago for the story of this contraband trade to matter, but one had to keep 'mum' in those times about many things.* [85]

Getting the contraband rum to the thirsty patrons of Millers Point was a risky business, however, and the rumours persist around The Point that the labyrinthine stone cellars beneath the Hero of Waterloo Hotel contained a concealed entrance, from which 'a smuggler's tunnel had been dug 150 yards through soft Sydney sandstone to Darling Harbour'. This tunnel was reputedly also used for the 'involuntary recruitment of sailors'. By means of a trapdoor a drunken reveller would be spirited below to the cellars and would awake next morning shanghaied aboard a wool clipper or 'cutting up blubber on a year's whaling cruise'.[86] Fanciful embellishment on fact surrounded such stories, but there is no doubt that desertion of crews and shanghaiing did take place. In May 1838, the masters of fourteen of these vessels reported that 106 of their crew were missing. Despite myths to the contrary, most native-born Australians were reluctant to go to sea, perhaps because of the harsh discipline and the 'convict' associations it entailed, and there was among them a high incidence of absconding.[87] Indeed, among the professional seafarers of Millers Point, there was a notable predominance of Englishmen, Scandinavians and other

---

85 *Evening News*, 3 August 1905.
86 *SMH*, 11 April 1989; 'The Hero of Waterloo 1843' (pamphlet, nd, available at the hotel); ML SLNSW newspaper cuttings, Vol 6, p 108.
87 Alan Atkinson and Marian Aveling, *Australians 1838* (Fairfax Syme & Weldon Associates, Sydney, 1987), p 141; Portia Robinson, *The Hatch and Brood of Time: A Study of the First Generation of Native-Born Australians 1788–1828* (Oxford University Press, Melbourne, 1985), Vol 1, pp 237–38.

'foreigners' as both officers and crews. In 1847, a Portuguese crewman called Matts left an American whaler and hid for six weeks in the bush on Middle Head until his vessel had cleared port.[88]

> *There was no Sabbath on board a whaler . . . except on one or two occasions when the captain had got religious. But then it was never lucky, for the whales sort of knew it, and played round the boat all Sunday but never showed on week days. The forecastle was scarcely twelve feet square and not high enough to allow a tall man to stand up, with little or no light. Ventilation was unknown, except what might come down the narrow hatchway, and this had to be shut down in rough weather. Some twenty to twenty five men slept, ate, lived in sickness and in health, without fire in the rigours of*

Looking north across Cuthbert's shipyard in Darling Harbour. Note the fine houses on The Point.

88 *Evening News*, 6 August 1906.

winter or without cooling appliances in summer heat; their sea-chests, their hammocks or bunks their only furniture. Can it be wondered that men deserted to try a land life, even if in a country in which they did not know a word of the language.[89]

With crews scarce, the practice of crimping became widespread. The crimp was often a hotel or boarding-house keeper, with whom Millers Point was abundantly endowed, who would hide a sailor until his ship and his savings had deserted him and offer him as crew to another undermanned vessel. This meant 'longer shore leave for the deserters and it may have increased the sailors' bargaining power with needy skippers'.[90] In the forties and fifties the pubs of Millers Point were central to both the social and economic functions of the area.

In these decades Millers Point was a bustling, hard-working and sometimes exotic maritime village. Work and play were governed by the comings and goings of the deep-sea ships. The cobblestone lanes rang to the sound of sailor's clogs, the thud of casks and the clank of leg irons as a sullen band of convicts, fettered in pairs, was escorted down Windmill Street to Lag's Jetty for the short boat trip to labour on Cockatoo Island. Both night and day the air was full of the rattle of ship's gear, the shouts of sweating men and the stamping of carthorses and, in the background, the bleating of the numerous goats that infested Flagstaff Hill. And every breeze brought the smell of salt, tar and the all-pervasive whale oil.[91] The foreign sailors gave the place a cosmopolitan atmosphere. Groups of Tahitian and Maori seamen strolled the narrow lanes complete with shark-tooth necklaces and sporting a 'demoniacal aspect'. Although he feared they might 'run amuck', J.B. Martin remembered them as 'laughing, tractable fellows and hard workers' whose usual amusement was snaring rats with a noose or, at night, perfecting a war dance by torchlight. According to Martin, Robert Towns's 'frizzly headed Tanna men were a much more dangerous lot'.[92]

The South Sea trade and the whale fisheries had made Millers Point, but it would be wool that would come to dominate the deep sea trade and the working lives of many local families. In the meantime the onset of the gold rushes brought great opportunities and great problems to the maritime community of Millers Point.

---

89 Ibid.
90 Alan Atkinson and Marian Aveling, *Australians 1838*, p 140.
91 M. Barnard Eldershaw, *A House is Built*, pp 15–16.
92 J.B. Martin, *Reminiscences*, p 36.

Early Millers Point to 1850

This 1845 watercolour by Eugene Delessert shows Millers Point and the entrance to the Parramatta River.

A view from the heights of Millers Point along Lower Fort Street in the 1840s.

2

FROM 1850 TO 1900

The recruitment of crews to man the growing number of ships based in Sydney became more difficult despite depressed conditions during the 1840s. As always, however, there was increasing competition amongst the shippers for the experienced seafarers. Robert Towns complained to Robert Brooks, his London agent, that 'those fellows with only one ship can afford to bribe officers with higher lays [percentages of profits] than I can with twelve or thirteen'. The rush to the Californian gold fields in 1849 only made matters worse, as many people sought their fortune in America, many of them leaving from Macnamara's Wharf at Millers Point.[1] In 1851 the commercial and social life of Sydney was thrown into chaos by the discovery of gold near Bathurst. Seemingly overnight 'merchandise went up, ships were in great requisition, houses could not be got at treble rents and workman's wages increased'. By 1853 Towns wrote that he was 'at a final stand what to do [as] carpenters' wages continue fifteen shillings per day and neither masters nor officers [are] to be found for whalers'.[2] During the gold rushes 'workmen were scarcer than nuggets'. On Darling Harbour a partly built barque lay idle on the stocks for seven years for want of labour. When it was finally launched it was named the *Kent Street* after the thoroughfare it occupied for so long.[3]

Despite this period of initial chaos, the overriding effect of the gold rushes was unprecedented economic expansion. The discovery of gold brought a shipping bonanza to Australia as a flood of immigrants arrived and exports of wool and gold boomed. Business was booming at Millers Point. It was from Moore's Wharf that much of the gold bullion was exported from Sydney during the 1850s. In 1853 alone bullion exports to London exceeded £1.7 million in value.[4]

In 1852 the arrival of the barque-rigged steamship *Chusan* at Moore's Wharf marked a momentous day in Sydney. After years of negotiation between the New South Wales Legislative Council and the English government, the *Chusan* carried the first mail brought directly to the colony under contract. A gold coin was struck and a grand ball was held and people wept in the streets as they read letters from home that had been written so recently. *The Sydney Morning Herald* trumpeted the 'unspeakable importance' of the event. Typical of the gold-inspired optimism of the time the *Herald* proclaimed a new era of promise and opportunity in which Australia was recognised as the 'jewel in the crown' of the British colonial empire. In 1855 the first steam locomotives imported for use on the

---

1 W.J. Dakin, *Whalemen Adverturers in Southern Waters*, p 117; Evening News, 29 May 1911.
2 Sunday Times, 8 September 1901; W.J. Dakin, *Whalemen Adventurers In Southern Waters*, p 118.
3 *Evening News*, 14 August 1905.
4 *Evening News*, 29 June 1905; W.J. Dakin, *Whalemen Adventurers in Southern Waters*, p 115.

newly completed Sydney to Parramatta railway line were also discharged at Moore's Wharf and hauled up by winches via Moore's Road.[5]

Next door at Towns's Wharf, however, the business outlook was a little less promising. As well as being beset by labour shortages, Towns was having difficulty insuring his ships. His major problem though was the steady downturn in world demand for whale oil. In the late forties Robert Towns's speculative empire was at its height and he manoeuvred his ships around the ports of the Pacific 'like pawns on a chess board'. Exports of whale oil were declining, but Towns continued to expand into the South Seas trade in 1850s, establishing a depot at the Isle of Pines near New Caledonia. His ships sailed direct to China carrying sandalwood, turtle shells and bêche de mer.[6] Between 1832 and 1841 an average of between £150,000–£200,000 worth of whale oil was shipped from Sydney to London each year, but by 1853 this had fallen to only £15,500 in exports. By 1856, Towns still had ten whalers, but labour shortages and falling profits prompted him to sell them off whenever he got a fair price. In the late fifties, Robert Towns's 'Rotten Row' was a byword in Sydney and referred to both the smell and the unseaworthy state of his obsolete whalers that lay at anchor off Millers Point awaiting a buyer.[7] From the mid-fifties Towns moved gradually out of the whaling industry into the pastoral industry, property and finance. He continued to live and work at Millers Point until 1865.

In 1813 the Reverend Samuel Marsden sent 8000 pounds of wool to London and predicted that wool would in future be 'of vast importance' to Australia. In 1823 Commissioner Bigge said that fine wool would become 'the great staple article' of the colony's future exports. In that year there were two commercial houses in Sydney engaged in the purchase and consignment of wool but, according to Bigge, the growers of the best quality wool were exporting it on their own account.[8] By 1838 there were at least eleven firms handling wool exports, including Walker & Co. and Lamb & Parbury, both in Walsh Bay. In the forties and fifties many of the merchants at Millers Point doubled as wool brokers and shipping agents. Wool was Australia's dominant export from the mid-1830s and wool presses proliferated on the wharves of The Point. Aspinall Brown & Co., W.C. Botts and John Macnamara were all involved in wool shipping in Walsh Bay and on Millers Point itself it was consigned by Flood, Ebsworth, Moore and, later, Dalgety.

From the 1850s, increasingly specialised firms began to replace the general mercantile firms as the major wool shippers. The ships too became highly specialised with the introduction of the clipper ships that raced before the Roaring Forties along the Great Circle route to London. *The Cutty Sark* was the fastest of the wool clippers and the *Thermopylae*, which anchored off Dalgety's Wharf on Millers Point, was one of the most renowned of the China tea clippers. Many of the private wharf owners at Millers Point offered substantial rebates, known as 'captain's pin money', to attract the wool ships. On

---
5 *Evening News*, 23 July 1906; SMH, 4 August 1852; *Evening News*, 10 July 1905.
6 *Evening News*, 13 August 1906; D. Shineberg, 'Towns, Robert', *ADB*, Vol 6, p 295.
7 W.J. Dakin, *Whalemen Adventurers in Southern Waters*, pp 115–18.
8 Samuel Marsden quoted in Reverend James S. Hassall, *In Old Australia* (R.S. Hews & Co., Brisbane, 1902), p 152; J.T. Bigge, *State of Agriculture and Trade*, p 53.

Millers Point

This view of the Millers Point waterfront shows the solid mid-century housing that lined Lower Fort Street.

their way back from Europe the ships brought passengers and merchandise to the colony. By 1861 there were six large bonded warehouses in Millers Point (belonging to Towns, Moore, Walker, Botts, Macnamara and Lamb & Parbury) where imported goods were discharged.[9]

The yearly cycle of the wool trade was 'the heartbeat which regulated all other trades' in maritime communities like Millers Point.[10] Labouring work was plentiful in the summer months when 'the wool comes down', and jobs could be had unloading the drays, pressing the wool or loading the ships. Artisans were kept busy refitting the ships and the waterfront was crammed with sailors and carters, and with porters who touted for business amongst the passengers arriving or departing as supercargo on the wool ships. The pubs and boarding houses of Millers Point did a brisk trade indeed during the wool season. The shipbuilder John Cuthbert took over Lawrence Corcoran's shipbuilding yard in 1853 and it became one of the major yards in Sydney, specialising in three-masted

---

9 *Sydney Mercantile Journal and Free Trade Weekly News*, 12 January 1861.
10 Graeme Davison, J.W. McCarty and Ailsa McLeary, *Australians 1888* (Fairfax Syme & Weldon Associates, Sydney, 1987), p 201.

schooners and other wooden-hulled vessels. In 1855 Cuthbert built the 60 ton ketch *Spitfire* which was armed with a 32 pound gun and was the first war vessel built in the colony. At this time, he was a large employer of local labour, with 150 shipsmiths, anchorsmiths, sailmakers, carpenters and block and mastmakers working at his yard. By the late 1860s, Cuthbert was moving into steamship manufacture and his yard was capable of turning out vessels up to 500 tons.[11]

Throughout the 1850s the residents of Millers Point continued to pressure the Sydney Council to provide basic services for the area. One of the major problems facing the residents was an inadequate supply of water. Millers Point was the most northerly extension of the water main and even a slight drop in the water level in Busby's Bore tunnel would cut off supplies. In 1854 a petition to the Council protested about the 'extreme inconvenience' of yet another break in the water supply. Mr O'Connell of Millers Point complained that he had been without water for two weeks. As in the rest of Sydney,

---

11 Harvey Shore, *From The Quay* (NSW University Press, Sydney, 1981), pp 122–23; *Evening News*, 8 April 1905; *The Australian Handbook and Almanac . . . for 1875*, (Gordon & Gotch, Sydney, 1874), p 133.

the sewerage and drainage of the area was fairly rudimentary. Joseph Faris complained that his tenants in Lower Fort Street were subjected to the constant discharge of water closets from houses facing Princes Street. The stench was so bad at times that the unfortunate occupiers were 'compelled to close all the doors and windows at the back of the house to keep out the horrid smells'.[12] It must be remembered, however, that living conditions in Sydney in this period were for many people fairly appalling and complaints like these were commonplace—and Millers Point was a great deal better off than many areas.

The difficult terrain of Millers Point was still a problem for many residents. Requests to build retaining walls and fences were commonplace. The Assistant Harbour Master, John Crook, wanted a parapet wall or fence and a gas lamp installed to stop 'drunken persons or young children falling over the precipice' on the southern side of Munn Street. The City Surveyor refused, however, arguing that Munn Street was too small for such a large outlay and he claimed that any fence would only be torn down for firewood. He also pointed out that the only outlet from the street was blocked up by Mr Crook who had turned about thirty feet of it into a private garden. The residents of the North Shore petitioned the Council in 1855 about the steep and dangerous state of Pottinger Street where the steam ferry docked after bringing them across the Harbour. Despite their fears for their lives, the City Surveyor told the commuters to attend to such 'trifling requirements' themselves. Thomas Smith's houses in Kent Street were left stranded high above the roadway after yet another round of cutting down the hills in Kent Street. The houses were almost inaccessible and eight tenants left en masse after one of their number fell off the cliff to the street below.[13]

By far the most common complaint was the state of the roads and the most vociferous critics were the wharf owners, especially Henry Moore and Robert Towns. They repeatedly called for the widening and repair of Moore's Road, where they worked, and Victoria Terrace, where they lived. However, these are the statements of consummate businessmen and do not necessarily reflect the reality of conditions in Millers Point. They claimed the area had been 'notoriously neglected' for years, despite the heavy burden of rates they had paid out. In 1854, Moore stated that the roads were totally unfit for the heavy traffic of drays and carriages that serviced the Millers Point wharves. He claimed that 'the business of Towns's Wharf and my own are much increased by the large Bonded Warehouses for which we hold licences, and that the direct Mail Contract Ships land and ship everything on Moore's Wharf'.[14] The City Surveyor was quick to point out that as the roads led solely to their own private wharves, it would be Towns and Moore who would be 'principally if not wholly benefitted' by any expenditure of public moneys on the upgrading of Moore's Road. Henry Moore was furious when asked to contribute money for such improvements. He replied that it was totally unreasonable to require 'a few individuals, many of whom, perhaps, have but a temporary local interest, to indemnify the city authorities for the

---

12 NSCA CRS 26/9/70; NSCA CRS 26/13/1084.
13 NSCA CRS 26/19/882; NSCA CRS 26/19/969; NSCA CRS 26/20/1166.
14 NSCA CRS 26/16/385; NSCA CRS 26/13/1161.

Houses left perched above Kent Street.

performance of such an important public service'.[15] In the eyes of the mercantile gentry of Millers Point, the public good was obviously synonymous with private profit. Of greater significance, however, is Moore's admission that the merchants had no permanent allegiance to Sydney at all. Like the sailors they employed, they too were birds of passage blown to the colony by chance and by the vagaries of world markets. It was this innate assumption of separateness by the Millers Point locals that helped make it a village apart from the rest of Sydney.

By the mid-fifties, Millers Point was being advertised as 'a thickly populated and increasing neighbourhood' and as a locality 'free from the dust and annoyances of the city' with an elevated site making it 'always cool and healthy' and offering the house buyer 'a snug and lucrative investment'.[16] Three houses in Crown Road, probably the ones later known as Merriman Terrace, were advertised as having the finest views in the whole city. They had six rooms plus attics, verandahs and balconies, and in the yards were kitchens, storerooms, coach houses and stables. Advertisements for the more modest houses in Kent and Windmill streets and on the southern side of The Point stressed their proximity to the wharves and maritime workplaces and spoke of the 'profitable daily traffic in this improving party of the city'.[17]

---

15 NSCA CRS 26/15/157/; NSCA CRS 26/16/385.
16 *SMH*, 19 August 1853 and 10 November 1853.
17 *SMH*, 19 August 1853 and 20 August 1853.

During the 1860s, Millers Point was in its prime as a residential neighbourhood. It still retained the characteristics of a well rounded and largely self-sustaining community. In Windmill Street in 1861 eighteen out of the twent seven residents who had a stated occupation in *Sands Directory* were employed in the maritime or mercantile trades. In Millers Point as a whole, 58 per cent of stated occupations were connected to the waterfront. Many of the men without stated occupations would have been wharf labourers and coal lumpers, occupations which *Sands* did not designate. In addition, some local tradesmen, such as carpenters, may well have worked in ship repair jobs. The economic base of the village had always been rather narrow, and the maritime and mercantile sectors still provided occupational opportunities for all classes of people in Millers Point in the 1860s. Labourers, artisans and the owners of small workshops continued to work and live within the area; in close proximity lived the wealthy merchants and professionals, and throughout the neighbourhood were the draymen, shop owners, publicans and boarding house keepers who serviced the needs of the community.

There were just over four hundred houses in Millers Point in 1861. Since 1845 there had been a moderate number of quality houses built in Argyle Place, Kent Street and Crown Road. In Lower Fort Street an exceptional row of townhouses was built, probably in the late 1850s. They stand today at numbers 57–61 and are 'probably on par with middle class London townhouses of the period'.[18] Eagleton Terrace just up the road dates from about 1865. Much of present day Argyle Place was built during the 1850s and Kent Street in the late 1860s and 1870s, including Alfred Terrace, Hesham Terrace and

Looking south towards the Australian Gas Company's works in Darling Habour and the houses of Kent Street, Gas Lane and Jenkins Street.

18 Howard Tanner & Associates, 'Millers Point Statement of Significance', p 18.

Winsbury Terrace. These houses were matched by the provision of smaller cottages for the lower classes. In Merriman Street, Davies Terrace (numbers 28–38) was built in about 1865 in what was then called Crown Road. On the southern side of The Point, Bettington, Munn and Unwin streets were slowly filling with stone and shingle cottages, and Jenkins Street near the Gas Company's works boasted twenty two houses in 1861, mostly built of brick and slate. Stone and shingle were still the dominant building materials in that year, but slate was being used increasingly. The major change in the housing stock of Millers Point was the size of the dwellings. In 1845, only twenty eight per cent of houses had five or more rooms, but by 1861 this had risen to over fifty two per cent, and probably reflects the replacement of earlier simpler housing. In the same period the level of rental housing in the area rose to almost ninety per cent.[19]

Many of the residents' shopping requirements could be met locally. In the 1860s Michael Clancy was one of three grocers in Millers Road and bread could be bought from the carters or from Harris's bakery in Moore's Road. Boats could be repaired by James Murphy in Windmill Street and a suit of clothes could be ordered from John Griffiths, a tailor in Kent Street. For years, James Jobson was the local butcher, occupying the building that was also the Napoleon Inn. Coal and wool could be purchased from Duguid & Co. at Edward Flood's Wharf and, if the family budget needed a boost, it was a short trip to Charles Barnett's pawnshop which stood next to his brother's boat yard at the foot of Pottinger Street.

By the mid-fifties the temporary structure that passed for Holy Trinity Church was no longer to be tolerated and the merchants of Millers Point formed a building committee and commissioned Edmund Blacket to remodel it. The enlarged church was finished in 1878. The stained glass windows bear the names of many of the local mercantile worthies.

The reclamation of the tidal mudflats bordering Darling Harbour and Walsh Bay had been underway since the 1830s. The deep indentations that originally formed the narrow neck of The Point were gradually encroached upon. The irregular shoreline on the northern side was steadily reclaimed by Henry Moore and Robert Towns as parallel berths were pushed out in blocky projections into the deeper waters. On the southern side of the narrow neck both Cuthbert and Charles Smith, who acquired the site of Bettington's original premises from Captain Deloitte in 1850, had filled in the shallower waters with parallel wharves and short jetties. The original shoreline was slowly obliterated and, by the sixties, maps of Millers Point show it as a gap-toothed jumble of rectangular projections, the new wharves and jetties giving the foreshore an almost castellated appearance.

The building of the new jetties and the extension of existing ones had been in progress since the fifties. Early in that decade, Ebsworth's Wharf on the northwest corner and George Marsden's Wharf just east of Kent Street North acquired new finger jetties. In Walsh Bay, W.C. Botts, John Macnamara, John Lamb and William Walker all sought government permission to erect finger jetties or to extend their parallel wharves. As more space became available, wool stores and bonded warehouses were extended. By 1861,

---

19 NSCA CRS 17/6/10 (Gipps Ward Assessment Book, 1861).

Millers Point had six large bond stores, belonging to Towns, Botts, Lamb & Parbury, Macnamara, Moore and Walker, where imported goods were held for customs clearance.[20] And alongside these were the wool, coal and flour stores and a multitude of sheds and workshops occupied by blacksmiths, coopers, shipwrights and other tradesmen. There were numerous stables in the area too which added a pungent ammoniacal smell to the already aromatic air.

During the 1860s Millers Point was occupied by a 'hardworking, industrious people, all connected with the waterside working, ship riggers, sailmakers and stevedores, men then coining money, for times were good, shipping at its best and Sydney generally prosperous'.[21] From the 1870s, however, things began to change in Millers Point. As wool became an increasingly dominant export cargo, more and more warehouse space was needed. Over the next three decades, much of the small scale industry in Millers Point was pushed out and replaced by large warehouses and remodelled wharves. The specialisation in the cargo shipped from Millers Point created a correspondingly specialised workforce. At about the same time, the artisans and the merchant gentry began to move out of the area, and The Point became a place characterised by wool shipping and wharf labourers.

T. A. Dibbs.

One of the first casualties was Cuthbert's shipyard. The land was becoming too valuable to sustain such industries and in the early 1870s Cuthbert's yard was being crowded out by wharfage.[22] Dibbs's Wharves and warehouses soon spread over the site. By 1868 there were at least sixteen major wharves operating around Millers Point and by 1875 the foreshore was said to be 'entirely occupied' with wharves, stores and commercial premises.[23]

The 1870s heralded a new phase of intensive development of port facilities in Sydney. In Walsh Bay longer jetties were built at Dalgety's Wharf, and Macnamara's Wharf was also extended as the new Central Wharf by the wool shippers Gilchrist Watt & Co., under the management of Alfred Lamb. Prominent engineer Norman Selfe was hired in 1878 to extend Moore's Wharf. He overcame the 70 foot limit on encroachment on the harbour by inclining the three new jetties at an angle from the wharf.[24] When T.A. Dibbs took over Cuthbert's property he began extensive redevelopments. Three long jetties were built in about the early 1880s next to Cuthbert's existing wharf and over the next few years Dibbs negotiated successfully for the extension of Unwin, Wentworth and Clyde streets to join

---

20 Surveyor General's Sketch Book, Vols 5–7; *The Sydney Mercantile Journal and Free Trade Weekly News*, 12 January 1861, p 13.
21 'Old Sydney by Old Chum', *Truth*, 17 November 1907.
22 Harvey Shore, *From the Quay*, p 122.
23 *The Australian Handbook and Almanac . . . for 1875*, p 133.
24 P.R. Proudfoot, 'Wharves and Warehousing in Central Sydney 1790–1890', *The Great Circle*, Vol 5, No 2, 1983, p 78; *Evening News*, 6 June 1905; *Town & Country Journal*, 5 October 1878, p 648.

Above left: Cuthbert's shipyard, 1871—soon to be replaced by Dibbs's wharves. *Above right:* Ships tied up at Dibbs's Wharf.

up with his wharf roadways. By the late nineties, he had purchased from the City Council the ends of both Unwin and Wentworth streets. In 1879 he claimed to have spent £30,000 on 'improving the north end of the city'.[25]

By 1886, storage and berthing capacities at Millers Point had been increased to cope with a boom in imports and wool exports. Dibbs's Wharf could handle seven 4,000 ton ships at once and could store 10,000 tons of goods. Smith's Wharf was similar size and the older wharves like Moore's, Walker's and Towns's wharves were now dwarfed by their newer neighbours. Dalgety's Wharf had a 340 foot jetty, could press 2,000 bales of wool a day and had storage accommodation for 15,000 tons of cargo, which was handled using 'the most improved hydraulic lifts and wool shoots'.[26] The Central Wharf was upgrading its storage facilities to accommodate 30,000 bales of wool and Dalton's Wharf in Windmill Street boasted two bond stores and five warehouses with a total capacity of 35,000 tons and fitted with hydraulic hoists. One of these lifts could hoist up 'a loaded waggon with horses and men complete a distance in height of 35 feet to Lower Fort Street'. In 1885 it discharged fifty three vessels using the latest hydraulic cranes.[27]

Andrew Garran describes the waterfront as it appeared at night in the eighties:

> The shore is thick with jetties, alongside which loom, silent and dark, the bold forms of various craft, while elsewhere are steamers agleam with long rows of cabin lights, their decks alive with the bustle of departure. Passengers, porters and stewards throng the gangways; seamen rush hither and thither at the order of the officer pacing the bridge,

---

25 NSCA CRS 26/155/13; NSCA CRS 3/10; NSCA CRS 3/12.
26 *Docks, Slips and Engineering Establishments of Port Jackson* (NSW GP; Sydney; 1886), pp 17–18.
27 Ibid, pp 18–19.

and hurrying forward the departure; the shrill scream of the whistle breaks upon the ear; and the clang of the signal-bell ringing out upon the midnight air, echoes from the silent hills that skirt the water's edge upon the other side. Behind the long line of vessels is the background of the rising land, with the houses irregularly grouped, and the summit of the rocky hill—the Acropolis of Sydney—crowned with the Observatory tower.

The increasing pressure on wharf space in this period saw the disappearance of many of the small workshops and businesses that had been scattered in and around the waterfront of Millers Point. As these sometimes ramshackle sheds disappeared, so did many of the small but vital local services, like the wood and coal merchants, limeburners such as the Kennedys from Moore's Wharf, and timber dealers such as Henry Moon from Flood's Wharf. A more significant impact on Millers Point was the loss of the skilled artisans allied to the shipbuilding and repair industry. The loss of Cuthbert's yard to the advancing tide of Dibb's wharves was a major blow to the diversity of the local workforce. And as more wool stores were built, the smaller independent shops were swept away. One observer noted in 1886 that the rapid increase in commerce and the demand for 'new and commodious stores' saw the artisans of Millers Point being steadily 'pushed out to the suburbs'. Garran remarked that many of the fine old houses had taken in boarders, whilst others had been pulled down for stores since the 1870s.[28]

The local gentry too were leaving Millers Point. Like many of his colleagues, Henry Moore finally left Millers Point in the 1870s. During this decade protests from the well-to-do locals called the Council's attention to the implications of increasing traffic that plied the streets of Millers Point. The moneyed professionals of Lower Fort Street complained of the injurious clouds of dust whipped up by the horsedrawn omnibuses 'passing and repassing every few minutes' to and from the wharves and the North Shore ferry in Pottinger Street. J.L. Isaacs felt besieged by the large numbers of drays, carts and cabs as they left from their stables near his house to work down at the waterfront. By 1879, the City Surveyor reported that Moore's Road from Smith's Wharf to Moore's Wharf was in 'a very bad state' due to the 'great deal of traffic' it conveyed.[29] Both of the grand houses, Moorecliff and Spencer Lodge, had, in their day, proclaimed the power of the local elite, but they were abandoned by the merchant aristocracy of Millers Point in the eighties and ended up as utilitarian outposts of Sydney Hospital. The increasing specialisation in the cargoes shipped from Millers Point shrank the economic base of the village as a whole and caused a significant narrowing of the class structure within it. Millers Point was increasingly an area occupied by unskilled and semi-skilled employees who worked on the wharves—in short, wharf labourers loading wool.[30]

Despite the traffic, Millers Point still remained a fairly amenable residential area compared to the rest of Sydney in the seventies and eighties. From 1875 the residents of

---

28 Andrew Garran, *The Picturesque Atlas of Australasia* (Picturesque Atlas Publishing Co., Sydney, 1886), Vol 1, pp 64–65, 76; W.H.G. Freame, *Press Contributions*, Vol 2, p 104.
29 NSCA CRS 26/148/1194; NSCA CRS 26/143/32; NSCA CRS 26/160/1196.
30 Terry Kass, 'Socio-Economic History of Millers Point', p 17.

Wool shipping came to dominate the wharves at Millers Point.

the inner areas of the metropolis were subjected to a street-by-street scrutiny of the condition of their houses. Under the auspices of the Sydney City and Suburban Sewage and Health Board, an earnest party of reforming gentlemen ascended the heights to Millers Point in November 1875. Amid the rocky back lanes of the village they discovered an old 'iron shanty' in Kent Street, owned by Mr Glover, in which the 'ventilation in all directions [was] excessive' and visited a few cowyards, two of which still operated in Windmill Street, but found little else in the way of filth or dilapidation. The most dangerous nuisance they reported was in Clyde Street where the unfortunate tenants of James Campbell's houses had to endure the frightful stench of the water-closets he had carelessly located beneath the steps that led to the houses. At Numbers 14–16 Clyde Street, one water-closet did duty for twenty persons. These were the most heinous of the few complaints levelled against the whole village and, by the standards of Victorian Sydney, such sanitary transgressions were more often the rule than the exception. In Windmill Street the houses 'chiefly occupied by the families of seafaring men and mechanics appeared to be clean, well conducted and not badly ventilated'. On The Point itself they were delighted to report there were thirty new houses which were 'all well drained and with closets fitted up with cisterns in accordance with the new regulations'. The new houses in Merriman Street were clean and well ventilated and the only 'shanty' they could lay their hands upon, in Smith's Paddock, presumably at the end of Bettington Street, proved to be 'the picture of neatness'.[31]

These reports were a remarkable commendation of the relatively good health and housing that prevailed in Millers Point. Other less fortunate areas, like Darling Harbour

---

31 SCSSHB, Eleventh Progress Report, *NSW V&P*, LA, 1875–76, Vol 5, pp 558, 565.

south, Surry Hills and The Rocks, were damned unreservedly by the Board in twelve mammoth reports that exposed the sunless squalor and poverty of these archetypal slums. The whole process was repeated in the 1880s by the City of Sydney Improvement Board which, besides condemning three stone houses in Hart Street—'Inmates very dirty'—found little else in Millers Point that warranted censure or demolition.[32]

In 1879 the freeholders of Kent Street North humbly petitioned Lord Mayor Roberts to have the north end of the thoroughfare renamed Loftus Street because 'the disrespect which the press and public attach (in many cases unduly) to Kent Street, does not apply in any respect to Kent Street North, and is found to be very prejudicial to the valuable properties erected there [and] because this portion of Kent Street has become an important mercantile avenue and one of the most frequented portions of the city, being the principal highway to the Millers Point Wharves and the route to the mail steamers of the International Lines, and is used very much as a fashionable drive.' Despite the social eminence of the petitioners the Council denied their pleas to be distinguished from the smoky factories and the denizens of southern Kent Street.[33]

In this period of official vigilance there were, however, plenty of warning signs of the future health calamities that would be visited upon Sydney. In December 1876 a man died from smallpox aboard the mail steamer *Brisbane* after it had arrived from 'northern ports'. Early the next year, a constable stood guard outside the house occupied by the Holden family on Summerbell's Wharf in Walsh Bay. The house was quarantined and the daughter of the family was buried at the Quarantine Station on North Head after dying of smallpox. George Dansey, the City Health Officer, warned the Council of the dangers of 'rapid communication by steam with foreign lands', facilitating the transmission of disease by the crews, passengers and cargo. He also pointed to the alarming risks faced by people living or working amidst the 'impregnated atmosphere' and the 'poisonous gasses given off at the principal wharves'.[34] Although his knowledge of disease transmission was, like that of most of his contemporaries, fairly primitive, Dansey's predictions about the state of the wharves and the control of overseas shipping would be tragically realised when bubonic plague hit Sydney in 1900.

Despite the changes being wrought on the economic and social structures of the area, quality housing was still being built in the early 1880s. Carlson Terrace at numbers 110–114 Kent Street is a well proportioned late Victorian structure built in 1882. Perhaps the finest example from this period is the 'beautifully restrained' Milton Terrace at numbers 1–19 Lower Fort Street which was erected in 1880. Lower Fort Street was still a fashionable quarter of the city and boasted many 'tastefully-designed dwellings'.[35] Numbers 36–44 Argyle Place, built around 1890, are a typical row of Victorian terraces and at numbers 63–65 Lower Fort Street stands a pair of Queen Anne revival houses built about the same time.[36]

---

32 *Daily Telegraph*, 7 November 1883.
33 NSCA CRS 26/159/956
34 NSCA CRS 26/143/21; NSCA CRS 26/144/299.
35 Ruth Park, *The Companion Guide to Sydney*, p 39; Gibbs Shallard & Co., *Illustrated Guide to Sydney and its Suburbs* (Gibbs Shallard & Co., Sydney, 1882), p 24.
36 Howard Tanner & Associates, 'Millers Point Statement of Significance', p 21; Royal Australian Institute of Architects (NSW), *Photographic Guide to the Architecture of Sydney*: Map Guide 1.

From 1850 to 1900

Millers Point in the 1870s.

Perhaps a more significant sign of the times in Millers Point was the erection of the Kent Street Model Lodging House in 1882. This philanthropic enterprise was intended as an alternative to the dosshouses and six penny lodging houses that attracted many of the migratory workers and sailors in the area. But at ninepence a night the venture was never a success during the nineteenth century.[37] Less philanthropic, but equally significant was the building of Stevens's Tenement Houses at 73 Windmill Street in 1900. Although built outside the 'boom' period, it is a classic example of 'boom' style architecture, with 'rendered classical details rising to a scroll pediment'. It was built by J.M. Stevens whose family for many years ran the Hit or Miss Hotel which in the 1880s stood two doors away from the Hero of Waterloo and next door to the Live and Let Live Hotel. Stevens's building contained eight apartments and is a rare and very early example of purpose built flat development in Sydney.[38]

By 1882 the Sisters of St Joseph were instructing the 200 pupils of St Brigid's school who had a great lack of playground space. They also cared for children in an orphanage attached to the newly built St Michael's church, near the corner of Lower Fort Street and Cumberland Street. This site, close to where the Harbour View Hotel now stands, was later obliterated by the Harbour Bridge. At the Holy Trinity school there were 210 children in attendance. In his report on Fort Street School, the Mayor John Harris stated that the building was 'utterly incapable of accommodating all the pupils, and consequently cold

---

37 A.J.C. Mayne, *Fever, Squalor and Vice: Sanitation and Social Policy in Victorian Sydney* (University of Queensland Press, St Lucia, 1982), pp 153–55.
38 Howard Tanner & Associates, 'Millers Point Statement of Significance', p 21; J. S. N. Wheeler, 'Old Millers Point, Sydney', pp 315–16.

lavatories and play-sheds have to be utilised as classrooms'. The Mayor said that the term 'model school' certainly applied to Fort Street's academic attainments, but not to its sanitary conditions, and the playgrounds were extremely rough and dangerous.[39]

Perhaps more hazardous were the roads of Millers Point. The great increase in traffic during the eighties turned the steep and irregular roads into a dusty, bone-jarring series of ruts or into a sticky quagmire, depending on the weather. The Council strove to keep pace with the work at hand. Argyle Street was woodblocked by 1886, and the newly wood-paved Kent Street was opened to traffic in January in 1890 complete with stone kerbing. Lower Fort Street and Argyle Place received woodblocking in 1892 and 1893 respectively, using funds allocated before the Great Depression of the early nineties had severely cut back the Council's schedule of improvements.[40]

Windmill Street was just one of the thoroughfares denied woodblocking with the onset of the depression. Progress was slower still on the more obscure roads of Millers Point. An interesting exception was the road that led from Moore's Road to Smith's Road, sometimes called 'Crescent Road'. In June 1887 the City Surveyor stated that it would be unwise for Council to woodblock it—'I warn that it is a private way', he declared. By August he had been prevailed upon to resubmit that report which now recommended, albeit reluctantly, the paving of the private road with cube setts on a concrete base at a cost of £1,275.[41] This was a remarkable change of attitude on behalf of the Council since the days when it quibbled at the requests from Moore and Towns to repair the public roads that led to their wharves at Millers Point. More fundamental matters were also on the agenda sheets of the aldermen at this time. In 1888 their collective sense of Victorian propriety allowed no delay in the installation of a six man urinal in the Argyle Street reserve. They rightly agreed that this 'would be of much convenience in the locality as there are in the vicinity cab and bus stands as well as other depots where numbers of men do congregate'.[42]

The most frequent and important congregations of men in Millers Point were those of wharf labourers mustering for work on the wharves. More than any other Sydney locality, Millers Point was the one whose character was 'formed by its relationship with the sea and with seaborne commerce that flowed in and out of its mighty harbour'.[43] And by the late 1880s the engine that powered that flow of commerce and the cycle of work was the wool trade. E.J. Brady was a timekeeper at Dalgety's Wharf earning one pound a week and a shilling an hour overtime. He recalled that 'in the wool season the harbourside is like a vast hive'.[44]

In summer, work was plentiful as a constant stream of wagons brought wool to the wharves where hydraulic presses compacted the bales, which were then hoisted into the

---

39 NSCA CRS 30/1/57 (Report of Mayor on Inspection of Churches, Public Halls and Public Schools, 9 June 1882).
40 NSCA CRS 16/29, p 108; *PC* 1889, City Engineer's AR, p 17; *PC* 1892, City Surveyor's AR, p 24; *PC* 1893, City Surveyor's AR, p 31.
41 NSCA CRS 16/29, pp 182, 194.
42 NSCA CRS 16/29, p 292.
43 Graeme Davison, et al, *Australians 1888*, pp 199, 201.
44 E.J. Brady, 'Personalia', p 41 ff (Letter to Brother Carroll, 21 October 1946), ML SLNSW. A3175; Quote from Graeme Davison, et al, *Australians 1888*, p 202.

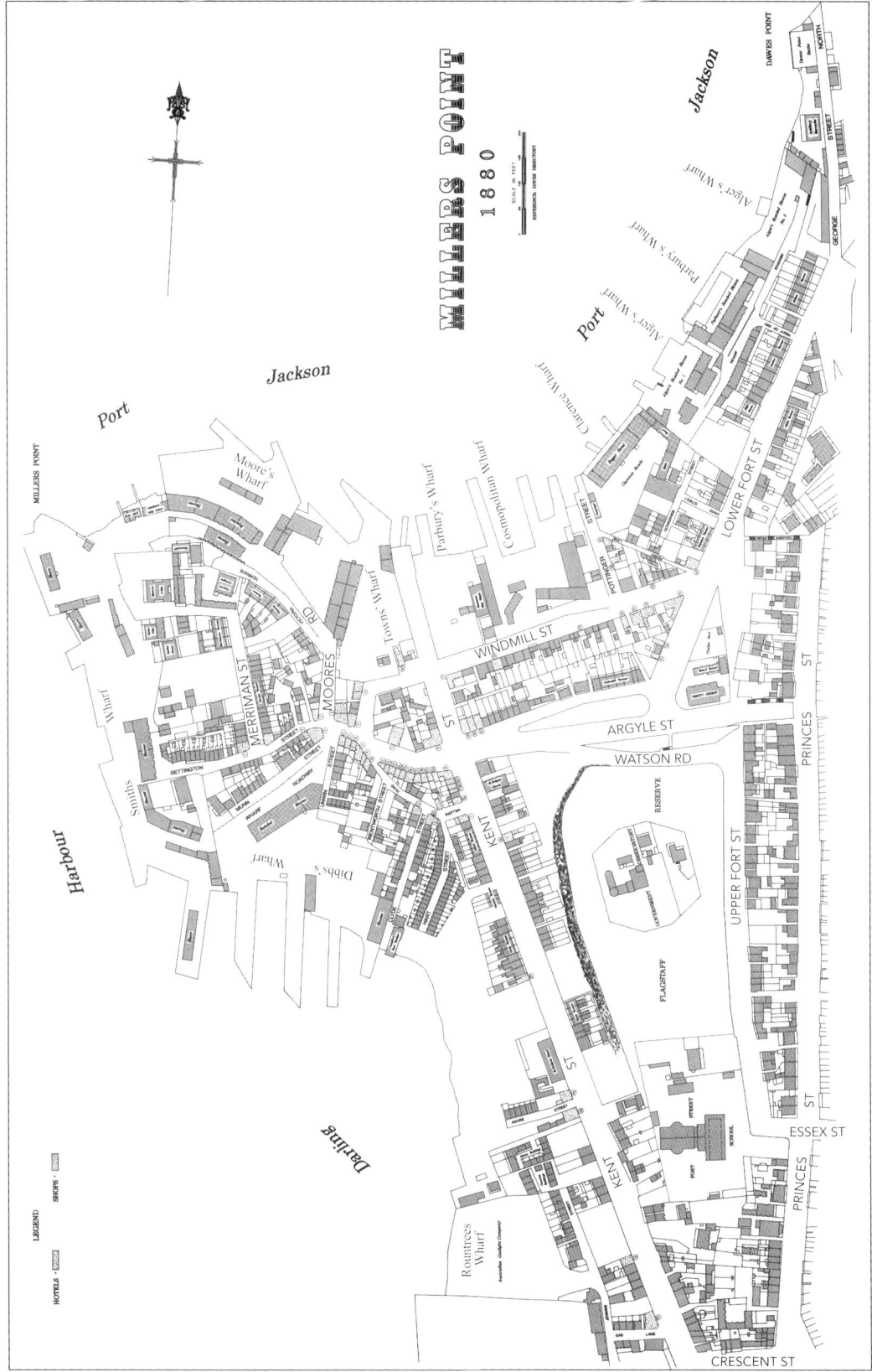

ship's hold to be packed down tight by wool stowers using mechanical screws.[45] Of course there were other cargoes to be loaded from Millers Point like wheat, tallow, hides, frozen meat and gold bullion, plus a wide variety of general cargo and manufactured goods arriving as imports. At the height of the wool season:

> *Stevedores and wharf labourers worked around the clock to keep the ships moving in and out of the port. Men reeled about the wharves red-eyed from lack of sleep; tally clerks nodded over their office table, while timekeepers and overseers worked until dawn computing time and wages. Once the season was over, all this feverish activity suddenly ended.*[46]

Work was seasonal and intermittent and the hours irregular. A shift of thirty hours straight was not unheard of and shifts could begin and end at any hour of the day. Ramsay McKillop of the Wharf Labourers' Union recalled in 1891 that he had seen 'pretty well all the men employed one day, and the following morning I have seen 600 or 700 sitting idly on the wharves'. In winter, work was scarce, especially on the deep sea ships that congregated at Millers Point. McKillop once 'walked the wharf for eight weeks and had to stand idle'. Conditions like these meant that the household economy of many wharf labourers' families was always vulnerable. Moreover, claimed McKillop, they paid 'pretty heavy rents' to be near the wharves so that they would not miss the pick up.[47]

Perhaps the most hated aspect of the job for the labourers was the pick-up system. The men mustered to a call for work and stood in a circle at the wharf gate to be picked up by the stevedoring firms. One wharfie remembered how he used to 'front up at Towns's Bond. Usually a clerk stood on the platform and sidled out the tickets. You, you and you and you too darky. He picked his men to get the ticket'.[48] This system pitted each man against the other and gave enormous power to the employers who could discriminate at will between the loyal and tractable workers, the 'constant men', and those they saw as too militant or troublesome, the 'spotted men'. For labourers who were out of favour, the going rate to bribe the stevedores to obtain work in 1891 was about two to three shillings per week. At this time the major stevedoring companies (many of them were wharf owners and pastoralists too) were Floods, Talbots, Dalgetys and Alfred Lamb and Co.[49] The wharf labourers of Millers Point were a hard-working and even harder-drinking lot. At Dalgety's bond store, E.J. Brady claimed that 'no-one was ever strictly sober after ten o'clock in the forenoon'.[50] The pubs of The Point did a roaring trade after, and sometimes during, a shift.

Many of their customers were ex-sailors or young single men. In 1891 in places like

---

45 Graeme Davison, et al, *Australians 1888*, p 202.
46 Ibid.
47 *Report of the Royal Commission on Strikes* (NSW GP, Sydney, 1891), pp 21, 23.
48 Waterside Workers Federation, *Sydney from Convict Days to the Eve of Socialism: A History of Waterfront and Waterside Unions* (WWF, Sydney, 1956), typescript, p 74. Since writing this book, new research on the history of the waterfront has been published, especially by Margo Beasley, *Wharfies. A History of the Waterside Workers Federation* (Halstead Press, Sydney, 1996.)
49 *Royal Commission on Strikes*, pp 24, 35, 66, 105.
50 E.J. Brady, 'Personalia', p 41 ff.

Millers Point the proportion of bachelors was twice the city average and three times the suburban average.⁵¹ In researching the history of Millers Point in this period, one notable fact was the lack of material on the social infrastructure of the era. The lack of evidence of sporting teams, reading groups, school auxilliaries and social clubs may be partly explained by the irregular hours of work which precluded both men and women from participating in formal or structured social activities. Socialisation was unstructured, impromptu and had to be fitted into an unpredictable schedule of work. Within these fluid limits on recreational time, the pub and the home were the centres of the social scene and the hatching grounds of the networks of neighbourly support that helped to sustain and unite the community, especially when times were tough. The women of The Point were especially important in the maintenance of these networks. Beyond this informal process, the only significant unifying structure that bound the community together—the men more especially—was the union.

Until the 1890s, organised opposition to the shipowners had been none too successful. As early as 1837 a group of seamen and labourers employed in the outfitting of the whaling ships struck for a pay rise of one shilling a day. Whilst condemning the 'combination on the part of the men', the ship owners themselves combined and issued a manifesto claiming that any pay rise would only cause the crews of the overseas vessels to desert their ships. The validity of this claim seems unlikely, but lacking any mode of effective resistance, the labourers capitulated.⁵² In 1872 the Sydney Labouring Men's Union was formed by waterside workers, but it was succeeded by the Sydney Wharf Labourer's Union in 1882 when 1,000 'casual hands' were called out, bringing the shipping trade to a standstill. However, this degree of organisation did not as yet translate into significant gains.⁵³

In 1890 the union took action in association with the coal miners' and shearers' unions to support the Marine Officers Association in a dispute over their right to affiliate with the Trades and Labour Council. This dispute escalated with both the unions and the ship owners pulling out all stops in a battle royal over the fundamental principles of unionism. The Great Maritime Strike had begun and by September 1890 Sydney Harbour was 'as quiet as a far western lake'.⁵⁴ Amidst claim and counterclaim about which side was first to take an aggressive stance, the Wharf Labourer's Union refused to handle wool shorn by non-union labour, the ship owners advertised around the wharves for 'free labourers' and notices were posted up by the stevedores stating that 'all men working for us will be expected to do such work and under such arrangements as may be required by us'. As troopers and special constables escorted the bales of non-union wool from the Darling Harbour goods station to the waterfront, the battle lines were breached, stones were hurled and the ensuing riot was stopped only after a 'mad rush of armed horsemen' and the reading of the Riot Act.⁵⁵

---

51 Graeme Davison, et al, Australians 1888, p 204.
52 W.J. Dakin, *Whalemen Adventurers in Southern Waters*, p 53.
53 Shirley Fitzgerald, *Rising Damp* (Oxford University Press, Melbourne, 1987), pp 210–12.
54 Ernest Blackwell, 'The Effects of the Strike', *Centennial Magazine*, Vol 3, No 2 (September 1890), p 87.
55 *Official Report and Balance Sheet of the New South Wales Labour Defence Committee, August–November 1890* (Higgs & Townsend, Sydney, 1890).

Parbury's Wharf west of Dawes Point in 1895. By then the deep-sea ships were mostly powered by steam or by steam and sail, but the fast clipper ships were still common on the Australian run until well into the 1890s.

The union was smashed and was not effectively reformed until a few days before the end of the century. In Millers Point 'the wharves were alive with non-unionists' and many of the strikers were blacklisted by the ship owners and had to struggle through the depression of the 1890s with little hope of re-engagement.[56] At Dalgety's E.J. Brady was sacked when he refused to enlist as a special constable. He had begun as a timekeeper at Dalgety's Wharf in the mid-1880s and before long took charge of the merchandise department at company head office. He had read widely in history and philosophy and discovered the writings of Karl Marx. He recalled that this was, in a material sense, his undoing. He quickly discovered that:

> *Marxism and Merchandise make uneasy bedfellows . . . In the year 1890, to pronounce oneself a Socialist was to brand oneself as a kind of political outlaw, associated in the thoughts of all respectable, God-fearing, loyal colonial citizens with atheism, explosives, free love and other forms of wickedness. Either that or to be regarded as a lunatic who wanted to seize all the property in sight and parcel it out among the unemployed. So Karl Marx and E.J. Brady went about together in secret, and like Old Man River, thought a lot and said nothing.*

---

56 Tom Nelson, *The Hungry Mile* (Newsletter Printery, Sydney, 1957), pp 22–23.

> *That silence was broken by the General Strike of 1890. I was called upon by my employers to become a special constable. That a convinced Marxian could put a badge on his sleeve, take a baton in his hand and march to the waterside for the recognised purpose of beating up the proletariat was unthinkable. I declined—the only white collar worker in the city who refused to enrol. I could not go forth and crack the crowns of those hardworking wage plugs whom I had associated with around Millers Point . . . and knew to be decent men.*
>
> *Thereat I was decorated with the order of the sack—a distinction of which I am not yet ashamed. The firm even refused to give a credential. The doors of mercantile employment were absolutely barred against me. I became a marked man. To be a marked man in those days meant worse punishment than it does in industrial circles now. Not to put a glamour over it, I very shortly learned what it feels like to go without regular meals, what it feels like when the soles of your boots preserve but a nodding acquaintance with the uppers, and your only coat is out at elbows and turning a faded green.*
>
> *Naturally I gravitated into the Labor Movement . . . and found expression for my revolutionary resentments on soap boxes in the Domain. During the pre-election campaign of 1891 I gave the crowd plenty of Shelley and Karl Marx from hotel balconies and other points of vantage . . .*[57]

The strike, the blacklisting and the depression took a great toll on the financial and emotional resources of the people of Millers Point. Even for those able to get back onto the wharves, jobs were scarce and, with the union's power diminished, were open to all comers. Wool prices declined, foreign trade fell by nearly twenty seven per cent in the three years to 1894, mercantile business was 'generally dull' and wage levels slid. Twenty five per cent of skilled workers were unemployed and the level for the unskilled and semi-skilled was considerably higher.[58] All across Sydney, families were evicted for default of rent, while many houses lay empty for lack of rent-paying tenants. At the City Council the receipt of building fees in 1894 had fallen by fifty seven per cent from its 1889 level. Apparently less affected by the downturn was the Millers Point wharf owner, T.A. Dibbs. It was in this period that his money began bolstering the coffers of the Council as he bought up the ends of Unwin and Wentworth streets.[59]

The long term social effects of the depression on Millers Point are harder to quantify, but no less significant. The wholesale rout of the waterfront unions deferred consideration of changes to the pick-up system for decades. The injustice of the muster system, where the pick ups were dominated by gangs of 'bulls' or company men, was not replaced until well into the twentieth century. Many of the workers of Millers Point were politically radicalised by the events of the terrible nineties. Men like Ted Brady became the pillars of the labour movement, the ALP and later the Communist Party. Throughout the depression the hotel balcony and the soapbox in the Domain were the platforms for Ted's radical oratories.

---

57 E.J. Brady, 'Personalia', p 41 ff, ML SLNSW MSS, A 175.
58 *PC* 1894, TCR, p 1; *Macquarie Book of Events*, pp 205, 223.
59 *PC* 1894, City Building Surveyor's AR, p 7; *PC* 1894, TCR, p 16.

In the minds of many Sydneysiders, Millers Point also became more isolated from the rest of Sydney. The workers of the area and the union that bound them together had been vilified in the Sydney press and a judgemental distance was staked out between waterfront areas like The Point and the rest of Sydney. The reputation of the area as 'rough' stems from this period. Years later, wharfie Tom Nelson observed that after the 1890 strike the Australian workers understood 'that there was a capitalist state and [that] it had given them a thrashing'. The pain of this was long felt in Millers Point.[60]

Larry Foley, the famous boxer and sometime king of The Rocks Push. The Millers Point Push was not as large or as powerful as its neighbouring gang and was at times controlled by it.

The increasingly narrow class structure of The Point did not help its reputation either. To a nation that enshrined the family ideal and was beginning to do the same with the principle of home ownership, Millers Point must have appeared as a strange and potentially dangerous sub-culture. The much reported activities of the Millers Point Push did nothing to alter such erroneous assumptions. From the 1880s the Argyle Cut was, in the collective consciousness of Sydney, a standing symbol of the perceived, and sometimes real, terror of the larrikin gangs. However, this had more to do with The Rocks Push, which was larger and better known, than with their confreres from The Point. The wharves of Millers Point had long attracted what were thought to be 'larrikins and loafers', but more often than not these lads were nothing more dangerous than unlicensed porters touting for business amidst the throngs of disembarking passengers.[61]

By the nineties Millers Point was often stereotyped as the territory of the push. At the western end of the Cut the so-called 'Irish Parliament' of the Millers Point Push lurked menacingly, distinguished by their dudeens (clay pipes) and sporting white-spotted red and blue bandanas. Isadore Brodsky wrote in his description of the Cut:

> *The air of criminality hung round it, particularly after dark. Many an unwary seaman, as well as the ordinary citizen, ran the gauntlet as the crimp, the thug, the garrotter, the footpad, and the 'playful' push moved into possession. The gas lamps, with their yellow-green glare, spaced parsimoniously, conspired with these elements to produce an unhealthy civic station . . . The terrors of the Cut lessened sharply after the introduction of the tram service to Millers Point.*[62]

In June 1893 a sailor from the *Royal Tar*, Tom Pert, was kicked to death outside the Gladstone Hotel at the corner of Argyle Street and Moore's Road in revenge for Pert having

---

60 Waterside Workers Federation, *Sydney from Convict Days to the Eve of Socialism*, p 12.
61 *PC* 1889, Inspector of Nuisances AR, p 6.
62 Isadore Brodsky, *The Streets of Sydney*, pp 22–23.

The Millers Point Push on trial for the murder of Tom Pert.

caused one of the larrikin leaders to be gaoled. None of the attackers, who were skilled tradesmen or wharf workers, were convicted after the alleged intimidation of witnesses.[63] The reputation of Millers Point suffered terribly as a result of the killing of Tom Pert as did, no doubt, the beer sales at the Gladstone Hotel.

By the end of the century the streetscape of Millers Point was dominated by wool and bond stores. Dalgety's New Bond Store was built in 1875 and still stands in what is left of Munn Street. The Grafton bond and many of the Windmill Street stores date from the 1880s. In 1892 Alfred Lamb completed a new warehouse in Windmill Street as did W.H. Hentsch on the corner of Kent and Windmill streets. This latter store was burnt out in 1903 and was replaced by Oswald's bond store. Alfred Lamb added another story to the premises at Central Wharf in 1891 and, despite the depression, Dalgety & Co. built new offices on Towns's old wharf in 1894. In the same year Dalgety's completed another wool store on Dibbs's Wharf which they were also occupying by this time.[64]

Whilst these palatial stores were looming ever higher above the surrounding houses, the wharves of Millers Point were in a very insanitary state by the end of the century. At Dalgety's (Dibbs's) Wharf the jetties and building were in good order, but the seafront was a sandstone rubble that was a haven for rats. All the others had similar seafronts, except Dalton's Wharf in Walsh Bay, which boasted a sheet piling wall. At Moore's Wharf the urinals were 'very offensive' and nearly all of the wharves had 'water closets [that] drain into the harbour'.[65] Much of the harbour foreshore was awash with rubbish, tainted by pollution and infested by rats. In the 1890s there were numerous petitions to Council about the unhealthy state of the wharf properties in Millers Point. Any allied complaints

---

63 *SMH*, 26 June 1893; James Murray, *Larrikins*, (Lansdowne Press, Melbourne, 1973), pp 134, 136, 140.
64 *PC* 1891, City Building Surveyor's AR, p 12; *PC* 1894, City Building Surveyor's AR, p 3.
65 NSCA CRS 28/1690/1903/.

Local boys survey the damage after the huge fire at Hentsch's bond store in 1903.

about the unpleasant odours and danger to health arising from the wool, hide and tallow stores of the city elicited from the Council's Inspector of Nuisances a reply that these articles were vital to trade and that no 'coercive measures' should be taken in case it should 'cripple our commerce'.[66]

Against this laissez faire attitude of a business-dominated Council, since the 1870s there had been moves by reforming elements within government towards increasing intervention in the management of the waterfront. There had been much talk of schemes to extend government control over the wharves and associated rail networks, but as yet there had been little action.[67] However, this inaction would soon end when Sydney was struck by bubonic plague carried in the rat-infested holds of the overseas ships that came to dock in its harbour.

Millers Point at the turn of the century, with the Observatory in the background.

---

66 PC 1893, Inspector of Nuisances AR, pp 2–3.
67 Alan Roberts, 'City Improvement in Sydney: Public Policy 1880-1900' (PhD, Sydney University, 1979), pp 88–110.

Artists have been attracted to Millers Point as a source of inspiration. This view of Clyde Street was painted by Sydney Long in 1902.

3

FROM 1900 TO 1939

With the start of the new century came a ferment of change at Millers Point. Great moves were set afoot in 1900 which were to result in the sweeping away of old landscapes and old customs and the creation of new ways. Whole streets of houses disappeared forever, like Millers Road, Unwin Street and Hart Street. Munn Street grew longer, while new streets emerged—such as High Street which perched way up above the wide sweep of the new Hickson Road, down at the bottom of the cliff at the wharves' edge.

The old styles of doing business on the wharves gave way as the old wharves themselves disappeared and old styles of landlordism were replaced by government control. The people of The Point began to experience bureaucratic involvement in their daily affairs which was quite unlike anything they had experienced before. In the closing decades of the nineteenth century, the authorities had begun to take notice of conditions at Millers Point, but all that paled into insignificance beside the events of the early twentieth century when it became one of the most intensely governed and directed areas of the city. Many said it was overgoverned; some said it was misgoverned.

The honour must go to Arthur Payne, a van driver of 10 Ferry Lane, off Windmill Street, for triggering the chain of events which was to result in massive upheavals in Millers Point. Payne had the misfortune of becoming the first to be infected by bubonic plague when it appeared in Sydney in the middle of January 1900. It was widely known that the plague had been visiting other ports on the trading route to Sydney, and just a few days before Payne's diagnosis, the City Health Officer had written a long report suggesting ways of dealing with it, 'if plague ever should come to Sydney'.[1] On 24 January 1900, the Town Clerk received a letter from the Department of Health asking for watchfulness concerning the health or otherwise of rats captured by the Council's ratcatchers. By 26 January, Arthur Payne's neighbours in Kent Street and Lower Fort Street had joined him in the Quarantine Station, and houses and lanes in the vicinity of his Ferry Lane residence were being disinfected.[2]

In February, two more cases of the plague were notified to the Department of Health, and there were increased sightings of dead rats which had succumbed to the disease, transmitted by the infected fleas to which the rats played host. Charles Boyce, a solicitor of King Street, claimed that the secretary of a large steamship company had told him that up to two hundred dead rats were found on his wharves every day. The shippers, fearing disruption to their business, were concerned to keep things quiet, and in this particular case they dealt with the problem by shovelling the rats into the harbour.[3]

---

1 PC 1900, pp 309–10.
2 NSCA CRS 28/236/1900.
3 PC 1900, CHO Report, February; NSCA CRS 28/701/1900.

Children at the corner of Clyde Street, 1900. Several views of this street appear in this book (see pages 35, 72 and 84). The street was demolished for the building of Hickson Road.

The City Council increased its rat-catching efforts, but did nothing about this kind of practice. Nor did the Department of Health, which held ultimate responsibility for managing the plague. Even the simplest practices of rat-proofing ships' ropes or drawing up gangplanks at night were not carried out. It is easy to be critical of this apparently slow response to the occurrence of the plague, but given the widespread incidence of other more infectious diseases present in Sydney at the time, it is not difficult to appreciate. In January, when the first case of plague was reported, fifty one people had been notified as having typhoid fever, a disease which had killed over 160 people in Sydney in the previous year. By the end of March, when ten plague victims had been isolated and three had died, there had been 158 cases of typhoid and ten deaths. At this stage the potential seriousness of a widespread outbreak of the plague was being stressed in the monthly reports of the City Health Officer, but after a few months of worrying trends, the numbers of cases had subsided, while the hot weather at the end of the year brought a resurgence in the number of typhoid victims. This disease, and numerous infectious and environmental diseases in small children were of much more enduring concern, and claimed many more lives.[4] At the time, various medical practitioners gave their opinion that the attention being

---

4 *PC* 1900, CHO Monthly Reports.

paid to the plague was out of all proportion to the situation, and in the end it is not so much the initial slow response which is of interest, but the subsequent hysteria which requires historical explanation.

On 23 February, James Riley Dudley was the first to die of the plague. His premises above some shops in Sussex Street were quarantined immediately, and then, later in the day, after intense negotiation with the Government, a large area of housing and wharfage was added to the quarantine zone.[5] The next day the Council was informed that as it had no jurisdiction over the foreshores, the Government had taken 'supreme control of the immediately dangerous parts'. The Board of Health had prepared hundreds of notices for owners to cleanse their properties, but as the Public Health Act stipulated that the Council ought to do this, the Board requested that the Council serve them.[6] Thus began a program of systematically cordonning off areas adjacent to the wharves for cleansing and disinfecting. It was carried out under divided authority and generated a great deal of acrimony between the colonial authorities and the City Council.

Meanwhile, pressure was mounting for the Government to resume the properties and wharves which were affected, and on 27 March the Premier received a petition asking for this, signed by ninety members of parliament. After a lengthy sitting, Cabinet decided to resume the wharves from the head of Darling Harbour to Circular Quay, which included a strip of land behind the wharves about 300 feet from high-water mark.[7] Subsequent resumptions of other parcels of land occurred later in the year.

By the beginning of May, nearly one thousand houses had been disinfected and whitewashed by the Council, using the added labour of the residents, who were effectively imprisoned within the quarantined areas until the work was done. For this they were paid, as they were for rat catching, and it was easy for middle class onlookers to perceive this as a bonanza for the locals, but the disruption of normal work must have contributed to the strain on many household budgets. There may have been some truth in the allegation that hundreds of new 'residents' suddenly moved into the area in hopes of receiving the government handout of 6 shillings a day.[8] However the readiness of some to profit from the situation does not negate the probability of loss for the majority. The Sydney City Mission workers in the area reported instances of great hardship in the journalistic style common to such organisations, like the vignette that appeared in their Annual Report of the consumptive wife dying while the weeping husband exclaimed, 'No work! Yes the quarantining has done it. Oh no! We have nothing. God help us'.

The most disruptive thing of all was to be sent to the Quarantine Station on North Head. By the middle of May about 1,200 people had been ferried across the harbour and isolated because they had come in contact with a plague victim and not been able to conceal the fact from the authorities. Of these, less than ten had contracted the disease, and a deputation from the New South Wales Branch of the British Medical Association told

---

5 NSCA CRS 28/608/1900.
6 NSCA CRS 28/1125/1900.
7 NC, ML SLNSW, Vol 116.
8 Eugenie McNeil and Eugenie Crawford, *A Bunyip Close Behind Me* (Penguin, Melbourne, 1972), p 112.

the Premier that this enforced quarantine was a very heavy-handed way of dealing with a disease which was apparently not very infectious, compared with other communicable diseases which were currently killing people in Sydney. Premier Lyne was unimpressed, and the removal to North Head continued.[9]

Then there was the ignominy of it all. In his February report, the City Health Officer, Gwynne-Hughes, in advocating wide distribution of disinfectant and more rigorous prosecution of 'persons who persist in keeping filth on their premises', added that 'if those who worked amongst the wharves were stricter in their personal cleanliness, they would lessen the danger of infection [from the plague]'. In the ensuing months, as apathy gave way to fear and panic, many things were written and said about the unacceptable personal habits of these people—'people who do not trouble a bathroom very often', as local member of parliament W.J. Spruson put it. Wharf labourers' organiser and future prime minister, W.M. Hughes, remembered the quarantining of people as an 'unwarrantable outrage'. It invaded their privacy, he said, while the whitewashing and disinfecting ruined their pianos and sewing machines. Work was brought to a standstill on the wharves, leaving workers 'cooped up like fowls in a crate, exposed to every indignity and denied the opportunity to earn their living'.[10]

But clean houses do not prevent plague, except indirectly by reducing the places which might harbour infected rats or fleas. After several months of enthusiastic cleaning and liberal applications of whitewash, the districts adjoining the wharves possibly looked a little brighter, but the number of plague victims continued to rise. 'Experts' were divided over how the plague was transmitted, but it was not until emphasis was given to reducing the rat population that things were brought under control. Whether there was a direct relationship between 'ratting' and a fall off in cases is unclear, as the effective transmission of the disease depends on a complex set of environmental conditions, but undoubtedly it was more logical to target the rat than to harass the citizen.[11] By the end of August, when the outbreak was over, there had been 103 officially registered deaths from the plague, while minor outbreaks occurred in following years. But long after the panic had subsided the reputations of the people in the resumed areas were tarnished in the eyes of many. The actual disruption to their lives, already made difficult by years of depression, continued for many years.

As the plague receded, questions multiplied about the intentions of the Government for the area in the long term. The resumptions had been extensive, while the infrastructure required for administering the area was not in place. There was much loose talk about slum clearance and remodelling, but little action.

The conventional wisdom about these resumptions is that they were made in response to the plague, but the evidence indicates a more complex set of reasons. While there can

---

9 Sydney City Mission AR 1900; *SMH*, 18 May 1900.
10 *PC* 1900, CHO Report, February; NSCA CRS 28/821/1900; W.M. Hughes, *Crusts and Crusades* (Angus & Robertson, Sydney, 1947), p 174.
11 See Peter Curzon and Kevin McCracken, *Plague in Sydney* (NSW University Press, Sydney, 1989) for a discussion of the transmission of the disease. The underlying assumptions concerning the nature and meaning of the response to the plague are at odds with the present account.

Lionel Lindsay's representation of Dawes Point, which contained many fine buildings.

be no doubt that this visitation generated a certain amount of hysteria and caused widespread alarm, there were other reasons for resuming the area. In 1900, Gipps Ward, which contained Millers Point and The Rocks, enjoyed one of the lowest death rates from infectious diseases in Sydney, very few of the victims of the plague lived there and even fewer worked there. The area fronting Darling Harbour and parts of the business area of the city itself were far more affected, but here the resumptions were confined to the immediate wharf area. Neither was Gipps Ward, especially Millers Point, possessed of the worst or most crowded housing in the city, as we have seen already.[12] The Town Clerk was of the opinion that it was 'the seizing of a political opportunity more than the safeguarding of the city's welfare which motivated the Government'. As the Council was forced to take the brunt of criticism for the outbreak of the plague, it had every reason to be critical of the Government, but it can readily be argued that the plague did provide the state with the excuse it needed to justify such an extensive resumption.

The first and most pressing reason was the redevelopment of the wharf facilities to bring them up to international standards. The petition which the ninety members of parliament had signed asking for the resumptions had been couched in terms of the need to control the plague, but the wording was vague, and stressed that 'it is advisable the Government should own this property'. Various groups had been lobbying for public ownership of the wharves for several decades, and in practice there had been an extension of control, but it took the disaster of 1900 to tip the balance in favour of state ownership. Private control had resulted in a motley array of shipping facilities ranging from adequate to appalling. The worst were the upper reaches of Darling Harbour, used by the coastal traders and more marginal shippers, while the overseas shipping wharves around Millers Point were more substantial. In addition, the scouring of the harbour was more effective

---

12 Ibid, pp 9, 24, 78, 92, 123.

here, keeping the water somewhat cleaner. Nevertheless, only a few wharves had solid seawalls, while most were of rubble construction, which was ideal for harbouring rubbish and vermin. 'Antiquated latrine conveniences' which discharged directly into the harbour were common.[13] The pollution of the harbour generated by the nearby congested housing can be glimpsed by considering the detailed head count of the scavenging boats which operated in the area. Between the beginning of January and early April 1902, they harvested a great deal of debris, including 1,252 rats, 382 cats, 539 dogs, 271 bags of meat and fish, 588 fowls, 25 parrots, 14 sheep, 6 pigs, 3 calves, 3 flying foxes, 1 goat, several rabbits and a shark.[14] By emphasising the worst of the wharves, assisted by graphic descriptions of their resident rats, those in favour of government intervention used the fact of the plague to silence any complaints about state socialism.

The decision to establish the Sydney Harbour Trust to administer the port's shipping was in line with trends in many other major ports around the world at this time.[15] The Trust was established in October 1900 and began operating under three commissioners in February 1901. As well as the administration of the port facilities, this organisation had control of housing in what was called the Darling Harbour Resumption area, in the immediate vicinity of the wharves—152 properties in all.[16] Control of these properties was

Cleaning up.

13 *PC* 1900, TCR, p 4; NSCA CRS 28/1690/1903.
14 NSCA CRS 28/1392/1902.
15 Alan Roberts, 'Improvement in Sydney' (PhD, Sydney University, 1979), pp 90–100.
16 SHT, *AR* 1901, p 28.

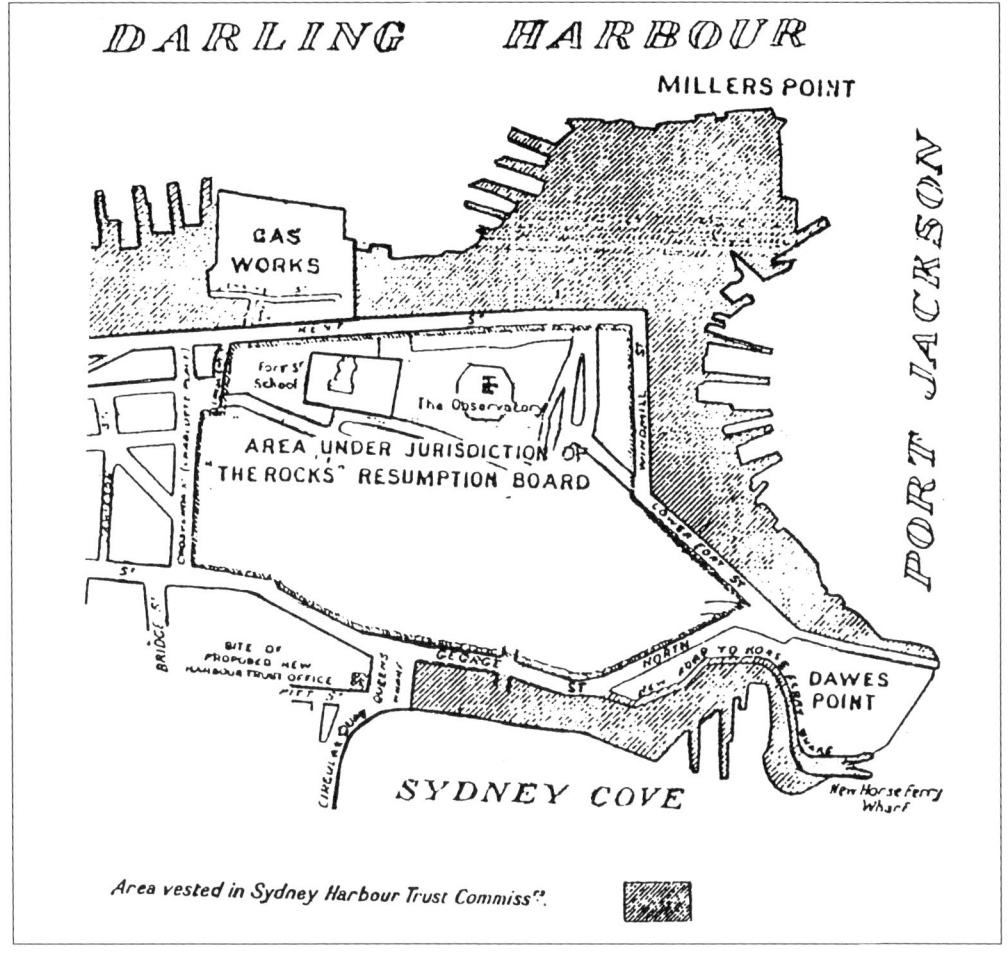

granted in order to give the Trust flexibility in constructing stores and facilities behind the wharves. The majority of resumed houses did not initially come under their control, but under the jurisdiction of The Rocks Resumption Board, set up specifically to administer what was known as The Rocks Resumption Area, adjacent to the Darling Harbour Resumption Area.

The need to resume housing for extensions and onshore facilities was bound to cause tensions, but the occurrence of the plague, and the ready co-operation of the press in playing up the residential inadequacies of the area only helped the cause. People who were familiar with the area knew that some of the housing was substandard, and that journalistic terms like 'rookeries' and 'backslums' were close to the mark, but they also knew that there was much fine housing in the area. The stock of nineteenth-century houses which remains today, almost a century later, testifies to the gross simplifications of the sensationalist representation in the press of conditions in this area in 1900. And in the end, when the final analysis of the location of plague victims was done, it was clear that Millers Point was not badly affected.

It could be argued that refurbishing the wharves was essential to plague control, but there is little evidence that this was the primary interest of the Trust. In the years following 1901, there were minor recurrences of plague from time to time, and in 1904 the City Council passed a resolution that expressed regret over the Government's continuing failure to provide for a rat proof wall in its estimates.[17] Eighteen months later, between January and May 1907, the plague attacked forty four people, of whom thirteen had died, and in February a public meeting sent a deputation of business and labour organisations, headed by the Lord Mayor, to urge upon the Premier the completion of the sea wall around Darling Harbour.[18] The Premier instructed the Harbour Trust Commissioners to let other works stand over and funds be diverted to constructing the wall, but by then there must have been many people who questioned the seriousness of the 1900 claims that the resumptions were carried out with plague eradication as the main aim.

R.R.P. Hickson, Chairman, Sydney Harbour Trust, 1901–12.

The second reason for the resumptions was to facilitate construction of a bridge connecting Sydney to the North Shore. This reason was easily forgotten when these plans did not come to fruition for several more decades, but in 1900 any of the residents could have ascertained the Government's plans for their streets from the press. In January 1902, for instance, *The Daily Telegraph* published a map of a new street plan for the area, superimposed on the old ones, with Princes Street 130 feet wide, 'to carry the proposed North Shore railway . . . and also for approaches to the contemplated bridge over the harbour'.[19]

Talk of a bridge was almost as old as white settlement in Sydney, but it had been on and off the agenda, more or less seriously, since the 1880s. Plans were considered in 1890, and in 1898 a select committee of parliament considered more proposals. The City Council was sufficiently convinced of its likely building to have a clause inserted in the proposed bill which would ensure that they could impose a rate on the portion of the bridge and its approaches which encroached on any streets or city land.[20] One effect of the resumption was to negate any requirement for the Government to pay such rates, and the Darling Harbour Wharf Resumption Act of 1900 specified that no compensation would be made to the Council for 'taking, closing or obstruction of any public way'.

In January 1900, the Department of Public Works had called for competitive designs for a bridge, and at this stage J.J.C. Bradfield, whose name is linked with the bridge that was eventually built, was already employed in the Department's engineering section,

---

17 RC, 5 August 1905.
18 PC, 1907 TCR, 1907, pp 10–11.
19 *Daily Telegraph*, 7 January 1902.
20 NSCA CRS 16/90.

working on the designs submitted. The advisory board, which was set up to consider the plans, was chaired by R.R.P. Hickson, who became the chair of the Harbour Trust in the following year. Twenty four schemes were submitted, and in 1903 the design of Norman Selfe for J. Stewart and Company was recommended by the Board. A change of government and a minor recession followed, and the scheme was dropped, and it was not until 1922 that the Bridge Act was finally passed, but in the intervening years there continued to be a steady flow of royal commissions, schemes and committees concerned with the project.[21] There was no bridge in the immediate aftermath of the resumptions of 1900, but the intention was there.

The Government's resumptions had not gone uncriticised in parliament, with George Reid accusing it of 'simply placing their paw upon a great area of Sydney' while ensuring that the Council could not 'carry out that sort of buccaneering business'.[22]

The resumptions resulted in uneven rewards and costs to the landholders. The land owned by the Garrison Church was exempt from purchase, but the rectory in Princes Street, The Rocks, was resumed. The payment for this property was substantial enough to allow for the construction of a handsome Edwardian terrace of four houses in Lower Fort Street behind the church. One became the new rectory and the other three joined the mere handful of privately owned buildings in Millers Point. Joyce Phillips' great grandmother who ran a boarding house in Essex Street received no direct compensation, but was given a house in the newly built High Street, rent free for the number of years equivalent to the assessed value of the Essex Street property. Thereafter she paid rent, taking in washing and cooking for ships captains to make ends meet. Molly Connaghan was born in Kent Street in 1902, in a house owned by her grandmother, but the family had to move soon afterwards because the property had been resumed. Her grandmother was paid £300 for the house, and as Molly tells it, she

> took it up town and put it in a bank. There were no Government banks then. She put it in old Abigail's bank, he was the solicitor. And then in a couple of weeks he went broke and she never saw a penny of her money. And she'd sit down and cry and curse him and call him names. She never got a penny of it. But she used to often say when she was short, 'There's that Abigail. He had all gold teeth. That's some of my gold in his teeth.' [23]

If the fortunes of landowners were made uncertain by the resumption process, for property renters—and that was what the majority of residents were—the situation was more clear cut. The inevitable disruption and financial loss caused by the forced relocation was exacerbated by the diminishing stock of housing in the area. For many, there was no choice but to find accommodation elsewhere.

---

21 Richard Raxworthy, *The Unreasonable Man: The Life and Works of J.J.C. Bradfield* (Hale & Iremonger, Sydney, 1989), pp 34–39.
22 *NSW PD*, LA, 1900, Vol civ, p 1137.
23 Trish FitzSimons, *'The Point's Changed a Terrible Lot'—Memories of The Rocks and Millers Point* (Randwick TAFE Outreach, 1988), pp 21–22.

The City Council was the public body most interested in the fact of the resumptions, and it would not be going too far to say that it was outraged. It had for many years attempted to gain the right to resume and rebuild housing, arguing that this was a municipal function held by councils in Britain and elsewhere. The areas which had been suggested for 'improvement' had included The Rocks, and from the Council's point of view, the Government was usurping its rightful role in causing this resumption in 1900. Furthermore, it was felt that the Government's resumption had been indiscriminate and heavy handed, taking the good buildings with the bad, and doing it in the context of a deliberate campaign of blaming the Council for all the sanitary ills of the area. There was a history of confrontation between the City Council and the Government, but nothing could quite match the animosity which was generated between the two levels of Government over the question of the plague. The press, which the Mayor claimed was 'daily shrieking against us', was overwhelmingly concerned to highlight municipal failings, so that when it came to describing the city housing 'nothing was lost in the telling', according to the Town Clerk, while the dreadful state of the wharves was 'touched with a gentle hand'.[24] The wharves, being past the high water mark, were outside the Council's jurisdiction, and again, were something which the Council had been trying to gain control over for many years.

Consequently, the Council engaged in a campaign of petitioning the Government to allow it to take over the area of The Rocks resumption. This did not include the areas controlled by the Harbour Trust, but it did include parts of Millers Point. In any case, the frequency with which the Government adjusted the areas controlled by the different authorities responsible for the resumptions made it difficult for the lay person to know just who was responsible for what.

In 1903, the Council offered to purchase the Observatory Hill resumption area, which included part of Millers Point, and it again made this offer in 1905. Lord Mayor Taylor claimed that the Premier recognised that 'the project of reconstruction came more properly within the scope of Municipal than Government enterprise' and after protracted negotiations, the Government agreed to sell as much land as was valued up to a maximum of one million pounds. The Council, however, had been arguing for the right to take over the area piecemeal, which the Government feared could result in it taking the best while leaving the problem areas. Also, the Government wanted to reserve the right to re-resume any land required for the bridge at cost price, yet was not prepared to say when this would happen or which areas it might affect. This left the Council in an impossible position, and it decided not to 'lay itself open to the suspicion of rash finance'. A round of haggling over a reduced amount in the following year also came to nothing.[25]

The Council continued to deplore the fact of the resumptions, but thereafter concentrated its efforts towards lobbying for more action, more improvements and in particular, for workers' housing to replace the houses which had been demolished. In August 1900, in response to the first demolitions in the area, the City Health Officer wrote

---

24 *PC* 1900, TCR, p 4.
25 *PC* 1905, TCR, pp 72–81; *PC* 1905, LMM pp 325–26; RC, 3 April 1906.

a lengthy report on 'Sanitary Housing of the Poorer Classes' in which he stressed that it was 'impossible to escape the fact . . . that the poorer class of labourers and others must and will live near their sources of work'. And while he conceded that much of the housing in question was far from perfect, he argued that in an imperfect world, more harm might be done by simply demolishing without also rebuilding:

> A considerable number of low-grade dwellings have lately been demolished . . . adjacent to Darling Harbour. In each case of demolition, the inhabitants have been dispossessed, the total aggregate accommodation has been correspondingly reduced, and the pressure on existing accommodation in the neighbourhood increased. The people must be housed . . . I am easily within the mark in saying that there are at present in Sydney hundreds of dwellings which, in their abstract merits, one would like to recommend for demolition, but a full consideration of all the surrounding circumstances makes it impossible to do so.[26]

From 1901, the Council petitioned for land to build workers' housing, and repeatedly accused the Government of breaking faith with the residents, by failing to do so itself.[27] At the same time, erstwhile owners of the resumed houses became agitated by the time lag between

Most of Windmill Street, including these buildings, was demolished in the first years of the century.

---

26 PC 1900, CHO Report, August.
27 RC, 19 February 1901.

Clyde Street again. Where are all these people to go?

resumption and compensation payouts. Initially 'property owners thought they were going to have a fat time of it', but 'the Government simply SEIZED THE PROPERTY, COLLECTED RENTS AND SAT STILL'.[28] While this is undoubtedly an exaggerated view of things, the complexities of the resumption did prove trying, and in 1903 the Town Clerk claimed that:

> *The Premier stated that he was sorry the Government had ever bothered with the Rocks Resumption at all, as it had given the Minister more trouble than anything else, but it was thought at the time that something better could be done with it than formerly, and probably the Council would be able to improve on the Government. As a matter of fact, to deal with it properly would involve the establishment of a large department for this work exclusively. The Government had so many things to do that it had not had time to give effect to the plans and specifications prepared by the City Improvement Advisory Board.*[30]

The Advisory Board referred to here had been set up within the Public Works Department in April 1901 in response to pressure 'to advise the Government as to the best and most effective means of dealing with the properties resumed'. Its brief did not include the housing under the control of the Sydney Harbour Trust, and this split in authority caused considerable tension. The Advisory Board, working in conjunction with the Bridge Committee of the Public Works Department, drew up plans for a new street layout which

---

28 ML SLNSW Newspaper Cuttings, Vol 116, c. 1901.
29 *PC* 1903, TCR, p 20.

accommodated approaches for the bridge and railway, but there was also an emphasis on the provision of public tenement housing.[30] The Harbour Trust on the other hand, was not particularly interested in building houses, and viewed its resumed property as land to be used as 'sites for stores and warehouses as the trade of the port develops' and in its first years of operation its demolitions resulted in many people being forced out of the area.[31]

This difference in emphasis could not have been helped by incompatibilities at a personal level between the heads of the two organisations. The chair of the City Improvement Advisory Board was Varney Parkes, an architect by training and occasionally a Liberal member of parliament. In the 1890s his allegations of corruption and incompetence against R.R.P. Hickson, then Chief Engineer of the Public Works Department, had led to a Royal Commission into the affairs of the Department. The inquiry cleared Hickson, who became Commissioner of Roads and in 1901 was chosen to head the new Sydney Harbour Trust.[32] The different skills of these two men reflected the different roles of the two bodies.

The Harbour Trust's response to the establishment of the Board was to request that the Government transfer more housing to the Trust. This was done in June 1901 despite strong protests from the Board that 'no permanent disposal of the property in question should be made until at least a comprehensive scheme of improvements had been drawn up'.[33] This transfer added 401 houses, 82 shop/houses, 23 hotels, 70 bond stores and 45 factories from The Rocks Resumption Area to the original 152 properties in the Darling Harbour Resumption Area inherited by the Harbour Trust, while an additional transfer resulted in 803 properties in all. Seventy one of the worst properties were immediately condemned and the rest were rented, and although the Trust stressed the difficulties of collecting rent from reluctant tenants, it was almost certainly these rents which were the reason for the transfer. In the first year, rents added £20,758 to the coffers of the Trust, while expenses on repairs amounted to a mere £1,634. As well as spending little on improvements, this new state landlord, which had no intention of being a state housing authority, argued its right to charge market rents and quickly established a reputation for evictions. Questions in parliament concerning the social disruptions being generated spurred the Commissioners in their first report to a public justification of their actions. While they had 'every sympathy for genuine cases of distress', they argued that they had no right to allow the property of the State to be non-productive. There was no talk of providing new housing.[34]

Varney Parkes, Chairman, City Improvement Advisory Board.

---

30 'City Improvement Advisory Board, Report of Operations' in PWD AR 1902–03, pp 51–53.
31 HT, AR 1901, p 27.
32 ADB, Vol 11, pp 141–42.
33 'City Improvement Advisory Board, Report of Operations', p 51.
34 SHT, AR 1901, pp 28–30.

Commissioner Hickson, with cigar, surveying the work on the wharf retaining wall, 1907.

However, the transfer of housing to the Trust did not apparently result in the ending of the Advisory Board's interest in them, for in 1902 it produced plans for tenements for the Windmill-Fort-Argyle-Kent streets block, and also for Kent Street backing up to Observatory Hill. These buildings, which were planned to house about seven hundred families and numerous single men were to be five storeys high, and according to one report 'almost as architecturally imposing as the Victoria Markets or the Post Office'. The Board estimated that they would cost half a million pounds, though others were inclined to think they might cost closer to two million.[35] Models of the buildings were on display, and a public meeting was held with the residents, but nothing came of this, except that about a dozen houses in Windmill Street were demolished in January, and as many again in the next few years, and the land left unused for almost a decade.[36] By 1903 all of the members of the City Improvement Advisory Board had either resigned or been dismissed, to be replaced by others, including Hickson of the Harbour Trust.

Thereafter, the Board does not appear to have functioned effectively, and its demise was widely seen as symptomatic of a general administrative ineptitude. 'Old Chum' took time off from his prolific newspaper writings about 'Old Sydney' to comment on this present event: 'A certain amount of work has been accomplished and a lot left undone. Many

---

35 *Daily Telegraph*, 7 January 1902.
36 *Daily Telegraph*, 3 May 1902; NSCA CRS 28/2222/1902; *Sands Sydney Directory* indicates that new housing was constructed in Windmill Street in 1908.

heartburnings have been occasioned, much bad language has been hurled at the Government and many owners are left in doubt as to their exact position at the present moment'.[37]

The demise of the Board left the Harbour Trust in control, with some input from the Public Works Department. The task of the Trust was to rebuild the Port of Sydney to render trade more efficient, and it was granted wide powers to demolish housing if it would facilitate port developments. The first major works undertaken were wharf renewal for rental to private companies and road construction on a massive scale. Eventually whole streets would disappear as the cliff was cut down to form Hickson Road at wharf level, and for many years the area was to be blighted by earth works, derelict resumed land and buildings in varying states of repair, some barricaded up, some half demolished.

The City Council, its nose put out of joint by the whole resumption affair, lost no opportunity to serve notices on the Trust over the state of its properties, while the Trust often refused to comply, arguing that what the Council considered to be a 'nuisance' was

Constructing one of the bridges spanning the low level Hickson Road, here used for storing building materials. This bridge carries Munn Street across to Argyle Street. In 1910, when this photo was taken, the Harbour Trust had just completed building the shops on the corner of Argyle and Kent Streets and half the row of flats in the new High Street.

37 ML SLNSW Newspaper Cuttings, Vol 116, nd.

often legitimate builders' debris. 'The process of demolition is naturally somewhat unsightly', wrote E.W. Austin, the secretary of the Trust, in explaining why certain things were as they were in Millers Point, but with definitions of these matters difficult to make, and tempers running high, the Council was prepared on occasions to sue what it considered to be irresponsible landlords, including the Premier and the Harbour Trust Commissioners.[38] By 1904 the Government had thirty five tradesmen employed carrying out repairs demanded by the Council.[39]

But if the number of houses diminished, the available employment did not, and by now there were more men working in Millers Point than ever before, with those repairing houses being the fewest of them. In addition to the normal wharf work, the Harbour Trust employed 350 men in 1901 and on occasion required hundreds more labourers. Work was also generated by the construction of a tramway extension from George Street to Dawes Point and Millers Point. This line, which was being built early in 1901, would eventually provide more ready access to The Point for workers living elsewhere, but in the meantime it too required labourers. Up to one thousand men could be gathered at the corner of Argyle and Kent streets waiting in gangs to be called up for work, a fact which resulted in calls for the construction of a public convenience and a shelter in the hope that 'the men could foregather there instead of hanging about the public houses and getting into undesirable conditions'.[40]

This preference for sobriety in the work force probably explains why the Harbour Trust built a coffee shop in 1903—its first foray into building other than port facilities. In 1906 it built some shops on the north side of Argyle Street, but only after it had knocked down some older ones on the same site. By now, pressure on the Trust to provide housing for port workers had resulted in the construction of a number of buildings in Day Street, on Darling Harbour, but none had been built in Millers Point, though many had been pulled down. At the beginning of 1908 the City Council formally urged the Government to consider 'the desirability of erecting workmen's dwellings in Gipps Ward', and the possibility of transferring some of the resumed housing to the Council was once more being discussed by the Government. That year also saw the formation of the 'Gipps Ward Progress Association', which pressured the Government to provide working class housing for the beleaguered local work force.[41] Perhaps it was these moves which spurred the Harbour Trust into action, for in 1908 it commenced building twenty two flats in Dalgety Terrace and in 1909, for the first time, it stated that it was 'policy' to provide housing for waterside workers, although it continued to argue that much of the land was too valuable for this use.[42]

At this time there was much debate about the need for a public housing authority in Sydney, an idea which became a possibility after the election of a Labor Government in

---

38 NSCA CRS 28/1690/1902; 28/3283/1900.
39 NSCA CRS 28/1110/1904.
40 NSCA CRS 28/667/1901.
41 NSCA CRS 28/127/1908; *Daily Telegraph*, 19 September 1908.
42 SHT, *AR* 1909, p 7.

1910. Continuing antagonism between the City Council and the State resulted in two pieces of legislation in 1912, one of which gave the Council the right to build within the City Council area, and the other to set up a State Housing Board to build elsewhere in Sydney, but also in state controlled Millers Point.

Between 1908 and 1915 the bulk of Millers Point's new housing stock was erected by the Trust and the Public Works Department. Shops, flats and a restaurant were built on the corner of Kent and Argyle streets in 1910, twelve houses in Munn Street in 1910, the beginnings of seventy two flats in High Street, along with the Lance Kindergarten in 1911, and flats at 30–42 Lower Fort Street, possibly in 1915. Ellie Byrnes of High Street recalled the move to new housing:

> *I was born in 1908 in Millers Point. My parents were born in Kent Street and my grandparents came from Ireland, individually in the 1870s. They met here and remained in Millers Point all their married lives. They had a family of two girls and three boys and lived in 54 Kent Street. My mother married and settled in Hart Street where we were all born. Hart Street was pulled down because it was very old and the rats were causing problems. The people had to live with relations until the houses in High Street were built. Then as they completed a block of four the people were moved in. There were seven of us and we moved here when I was a small child 77 years ago.*[43]

When the State Housing Board was established in 1912, it had the power to build in the area previously controlled by the defunct City Improvement Board, but although it constructed a few commercial buildings in The Rocks, its housing program was concentrated in the suburbs. This Board was disbanded in 1924, leaving the Harbour Trust in control.

The Trust's stock of old and new housing was rented to people associated with the work of the wharves, and eventually, to their children. The large boarding houses, which served the more transient elements of the population, were simply leased to tenants who made their own arrangements for sub-letting the rooms at whatever rate they chose. These policies provided housing in close proximity to the wharves for the local workforce. The Trust did not provide public housing on a needs basis, but in order to maintain its own work force. Therefore, it can more properly be called state housing than public housing.

The outbreak of World War I marked the end of residential expansion in Millers Point, except for eighteen flats built by the Trust in High Street in 1917.[44] Apart from some demolitions in the 1960s, this housing, along with surviving nineteenth century stock, still stands today with minimal infilling and minimal alteration to its external characteristics. It is clear evidence of a substantial building program. Yet the material reality of what is there ought not to eclipse the fact that many houses were torn down. For the people of Millers Point in these years up to World War I, this period of building was also a period of demolishing and of enormous upheaval. In the end, less was built than was removed, in

---

43 'Point People', typescript held in the Heritage Gallery, St Brigid's Church, Millers Point.
44 SHT, AR 1908–17; Terry Kass, 'A Socio Economic History of Millers Point', pp 47–50

terms of residential stock; and although this brief foray into residential building created some interesting housing, it did not signal a major commitment on the part of the Trust to worker housing. In 1901 there were 473 houses, shops and house/shops in Millers Point, and by 1928 only 433, including 163 flats. By then, hundreds more houses had been demolished or were being demolished on the border of Millers Point to make way for the Sydney Harbour Bridge. Although the houses in Cumberland and Princes streets were in The Rocks, their disappearance would have put pressure on the housing stock of Millers Point, especially as it coincided with the onset of the Depression.

Also greatly diminished in number were the hotels. Many of those standing in 1900 were of ancient construction and dubious quality, and because they tended to hug the waterfront many were demolished to make way for port construction work. Wharf work is thirsty work, however, and eventually the Trust found itself building replacement hotels—the Dumbarton Castle (1840s/1908), the Palisade (1912), the Big House (c.1915) and the Harbour View (1922). In 1900 there had been thirteen pubs in Millers Point, but by 1928 there were six, with old landmarks like the Hit or Miss (delicensed) and the Victoria Arms now only memories.

Harbour View Hotel, built in 1922. The building of the Harbour Bridge beside it a few years later made the name a little fanciful.

While the number of houses and pubs declined, other types of building proliferated. The task of the Harbour Trust in updating shipping and wharfage result in a vast amount of construction work. Millers Point did not have the most decrepit wharfage, having experienced some upgrading in recent years, but the Trust's plan was to create the most modern facilities, which would be leased back to the private companies, with higher levels of rates and charges being offset by more efficient docking and loading operations. The first major work to be completed in Millers Point was a refurbished Dalgety's wharf, on the point itself. Bond stores and warehouses followed, and in 1909 the major cutting down of the cliff face to create a new road (Hickson Road) at wharf level began. In 1910 new finger wharves between Dawes Point and Millers Point were commenced, as well as Dibbs's Wharf, between Dalgety's and the gas company in Darling Harbour. These wharves were double decked, and connected to two levels of roadways: Hickson Road at the bottom and the high roads of Millers Point by means of a series of bridges across Hickson Road. In this way the original impediment of the steep natural shoreline was used to advantage to create maximum access to the wharves.

The purpose of Hickson Road was not merely to provide shoreline access to the wharves. By extending back along Darling Harbour, it would connect up with the railway

Left: Creating a new Pottinger Street, 1922. In Windmill Street above, from right to left, the Hit or Miss Hotel, Stevens Buildings and the Hero of Waterloo Hotel. *Right:* The new Walsh Bay wharves were numbered 1–10. This is No. 1, near Dawes Point, 1914.

yards at the head of Darling Harbour. It would also give road access to the Pyrmont Bridge and hence to the wharves of the Pyrmont peninsula. The great width of the road was in anticipation of the railway being extended to Millers Point.[45]

The wharves between Dawes Point and Millers Point (at what was named Walsh Bay in 1919, after the Trust's Engineer-in-Chief) were not completed until 1921, and it was not until the following year that a new alignment of Pottinger Street was constructed. The building of Hickson Road continued into the late 1920s, although the Millers Point section, up to the Gas Works, was completed by 1915. Several unforeseen factors contributed to the slow progress of the work. The outbreak of war in 1914 resulted in rising labour costs as marginal workers chose the possible excitement of the war zone over the grind of picking rock in Millers Point. Prices for imported materials rose, and the materials then became scarce as ships and goods were diverted for war purposes. In 1921 the Commissioners reported that the construction of the reinforced concrete viaduct connecting the upper storeys of the Walsh Bay jetties with Windmill Street 'had been retarded by reason of the shortage of cement', and that because of the high cost of steel, they had 'not seen their way to order the bridges'. Instead, they proposed to build them in timber.

A second factor which contributed to slow progress was the Trust's difficulty in obtaining access to the land occupied by the Gas Works, which obstructed the passage of Hickson Road. The Australian Gas Light Company land had been exempted from the original resumptions because it would have been unrealistic financially to do otherwise and, although its eventual removal was inevitable, the company was slow to go. The property was finally resumed in 1911, but AGL continued to lease it as progress on building up its new plant at suburban Mortlake was slow. With the arrival of war, work on linking the city gas mains into this new plant was stopped altogether, and in 1917 the process of dismantling the Kent Street works was halted and the plant brought back into temporary

---

45 SHT, AR 1908.

production.⁴⁶ This aspect of 'the war effort', and the reluctance of the AGL Company to go was a source of frustration to the Harbour Trust Commissioners. By mid-1921 they had still not gained possession of the land, but had been allowed to construct a narrow temporary road through it, connecting Hickson Road to Sussex Street for the first time, and they reported that it was immediately heavily used by port traffic to and from Millers Point.⁴⁷

Although the building of this road marked the end of major construction on Millers Point, the Trust continued to restructure other parts of the port, and some of the workers on these projects were no doubt Millers Point people, because the Trust's policy for its housing was to rent it either to wharf workers or Trust workers.

One of the longstanding legacies of the resumptions was the creation of great confusion over administrative control of the area. Early divisions between the two resumption areas and separate housing authorities were eventually resolved in favour of the Harbour Trust controlling a combined area. But as well as owning the houses, the Trust also owned the roads, a fact which further complicated relations with the City Council. Under the legislation establishing the Trust, it was not liable to pay rates, thereby depriving the Council of a lot of revenue, and the Council was quick to assert that it would not maintain the streets for which it received no rates. It was doubly aggrieved by the fact that much of the Trust's property comprised wharves and warehouses which were rented out to private concerns, thereby earning direct income for the Trust. A legal agreement entered into in 1902 resulted in rates being paid on some properties, but not on those used directly by the Trust, and not on unoccupied land or buildings, of which there were many.⁴⁸ The Council was obliged to collect the rates directly from the tenants without any recourse to the landlord, the Harbour Trust, a reversal of usual procedure, and a cause for resentment, with the City Treasurer being of the opinion that the Trust had no right 'to claim exemption because their tenants do not pay up'.⁴⁹

Nevertheless, this agreement did result in an uneasy truce and a plethora of processes was established to deal with the area. The Council did some minor road repairs, the Trust paid for it to do others, some individuals paid a weekly fee to have their garbage collected, while some collections were done by the Trust. And so on.⁵⁰ Whenever the Trust proposed to widen a road the Council was careful not to approve it formally, as that might have shifted the legal responsibility back to municipal control. On the other hand, the lighting of Millers Point by electricity after 1904 was readily undertaken by the Council, as it was anxious to establish control of the whole urban network of electrification.⁵¹

The mountain of paperwork generated by the process of determining areas of control in Millers Point testifies to widespread confusion amongst bureaucrats, and indicates that for the ordinary citizen bewilderment and frustration must have been common.

---

46 Rosemary Broomham, *First Light* (Hale & Iremonger, Sydney, 1987); Interview, Broomham, 1990.
47 SHT, AR 1921, p 2.
48 PC 1903, TCR, pp 307–08; NSCA CRS 28/2646/OZ.
49 RC, 3 April 1906, p 113.
50 See for example, NSCA CRS 28/747/1901; 28/3355/1902; 28/805/1902.
51 RC, 19 September 1905; RC, 14 June 1904.

By the time of World War I, the Harbour Trust was attempting to give the streets back to the Council, and so was the Housing Board, which administered The Rocks. However, a change in the rating system now meant that no rates were being paid at all by this stage, and the Council declined the offer, suggesting that it would only consider administering the streets if the Trust moved to have its act changed so that it paid rates. In 1919 the legislation was changed and rates were paid, with the expectation that the Council would take over control, but legal battles over claims and counter claims of money owned by each party got in the way, and the transfer was not made.[52] The secretary of the Carters Union complained in vain about the potholes in Dalgety Road.[53]

In 1932 for the first time the Council formally resolved that as far as the roads of Millers Point were concerned, it would do only minor repairs and provide for lighting, thus recognising what had been the actual practice for years. In that year the Harbour Trust agreed to pay residents' rates directly, and again approached the Council to take over the roads, but this time the Council declined on account of their poor condition. As always in politics, the rules of the game were altered to suit the players, and in the depressed year of 1932 no one wanted to take on the extra expense.[54]

The extensive redevelopment of the wharves and the reorganisation of shipping that occurred during the early decades of the century was one response to the need to restructure the economy after the disastrous slump of the 1890s. An expanded and diversified export sector was seen to be necessary to service a heavy overseas debt. Australia was going to trade

At the corner of Towns Place, early 20th century.

---

52 NSCA CRS 34/4794/15; 34/4974/15; 34/169/21.
53 NSCA CRS 34/3083/19.
54 RC, 24 May 1932; NSCA CRS 34/5770/32.

its way into a new century of prosperity, with the help of the new technology of refrigeration and encouragement to farmers to grow a more varied range of products for export, including meat, wheat and butter. This 'export surplus imperative, in conjunction with new shipping rivalry from foreign powers, gave rise to a preoccupation with efficiency and cost cutting in trade'.[55] And the new wharf facilities were nothing if not efficient.

But by the time most of these new facilities were operating, the anticipated increase in the number of ships, and expectations of a rising volume of trade had not eventuated since World War I had disrupted trade patterns. If an analysis of the overall developments within the economy were to be attempted, it would be necessary to discuss the changing value of imports and exports and the relationship between the two, but viewed from the perspective of the people of Millers Point, other measures would be more useful. For the traders, the type, extent and value of goods was important. Dalgety's, for instance, was directly concerned with the price of wool handled and the cost of shipping it. For the wharf labourers, it was not the value of goods, but their volume which influenced the availability of work. Nor were they concerned about the balance of imports and exports, for they were, in effect, the same thing. Imports meant unloading ships, exports meant loading ships, and the more there was of both or either, the more work there was available. There were preferences for certain types of cargoes as being less back breaking than others, and some cargoes attracted pay loading because of their nastiness (dirt money) or difficulty or danger of handling (danger money), but in an industry which habitually generated more labourers than jobs, the primary interest was in getting work—any work. And that boiled down to tonnage of cargoes.

Shipping into Sydney Harbour was generally slowly increasing until 1914, but the diversion of shipping to war work after 1914 encouraged the local manufacture of some goods, while others were done without, so that there was a decline in trade until 1920,

Ship tonnage was on the increase. Here the funnels of the ships dominate the new wharves numbers 8 and 9, Walsh Bay.

---

55 Peter Cochrane, *Industrialisation and Dependence* (University of Queensland Press, St Lucia, 1980), pp 10–11.

when tonnage of imports was only half what it had been in 1914.[56] After the war, imports rose rapidly, and so did exports, particularly of grain and meat to a hungry, war-torn Europe, but total tonnage of shipping did not surpass the 1914 record until 1927. And this success was a bit misleading in that it reflected a catching up after the 1926 general strike in Britain in the previous year had tied up ships in British ports and slowed trade to Sydney.

From 1928 onwards the total value of goods passing through the port declined and from 1929 tonnage also fell. In 1930 the wheat trade collapsed dramatically, as the effects of a major international depression were compounded by local droughts. Wharves lay idle and jobs dried up. Conditions on the waterfront remained tight during the thirties, and levels of trade did not reach 1928 levels until 1936.[57] Conditions for workers remained bad, however, as men from other contracted areas of the economy still frequented the wharves as a place of last resort in the search for casual work.

In addition to the devastation of the Depression, there were several tendencies in the shipping industry itself which contributed to the irregularity of work in the decades leading up to World War II. By the early 1920s, increasing size of ships resulted in fewer vessels carrying the same tonnage of cargo, so that in 1927, the year when tonnage first topped the 1914 record, it was achieved with 8,366 vessels, which was 1,776 fewer ships than in 1914. By then, the Harbour Trust was employing rockbreaking plant to excavate more deeply close to the wharves to accommodate the increasing draught of the ships.[58] Fewer ships meant a growing irregularity of wharf work, with more men being taken on to unload each ship, requiring a larger pool of workers who would at other times be idle.

As well as increases in size, the increased use of motor vessels resulted in less coastal and interstate trade in coal, and less coal lumping work. In 1925–26 the store on Number 10 berth at Walsh Bay was converted to the first inflammable liquid storage area in the port in response to 'the increasing importation of motor spirit', and bulk storage tanks were built, supplied with electric pumping facilities.[59] By 1935, eighty three per cent of ships entering the port were still coal burning, but these accounted for only fifty four per cent of the tonnage, as the larger ships were the first to convert from coal.[60]

But reduced coal firing of ships was more than matched by the increase in other uses for coal, especially in rail transport, and it was during the twenties and thirties that land transport, rail and road, triumphed over short haul coastal shipping. Inertia, loyalty and large capital investment ensured that these ships would not entirely disappear until the fifties, but their fortunes were on the wane from the time of World War I, and a decline in their numbers was clearly visible by the twenties.[61] These ships were the life and colour of the Darling Harbour wharves. There was constant jostling of the red and black funnelled ships of the North Coast Company, the black, white and brown ones of the Illawarra and

---

54 This and subsequent discussion based on Annual Reports, Sydney Harbour Trust 1914–30.
55 MSB, *AR* 1936, pp 14–15.
56 MSB, *AR* 1927, p 1; *AR* 1926, p 3.
57 Ibid, 1926, p 2.
58 Ibid, 1935, p 7.
59 John Bach, 'Sydney and the Coastal Shipping Trade', in Garry Wotherspoon (ed.), *Sydney's Transport* (Hale & Iremonger, Sydney, 1983), pp 51–62.

South Coast Company, and various others of smaller outfits, as they discharged their mixed cargoes of dairy produce, potatoes, timber, fruit, livestock and passengers.

These ships were worked by men from all over Sydney, but Millers Point was the closest residential area, and when work was not available on the international cargoes, especially wool or frozen meat at Walsh Bay or Woolloomooloo, or wheat around at Pyrmont, then a man might join the throng along 'the hungry mile' of Sussex Street. Many never attained the prestige of working the big ships, and mixed cargo work was all they ever did. It was not so well paid, with the first wage award of 1911 granting fifteen pence an hour for deep sea work, and fourteen for the Sussex Streeters. Nor was the process likely to yield as many hours work, because while an overseas ship might stay in dock for days while its large cargo was loaded by an experienced gang of perhaps twenty men, the coastal ships relied on a quick turn around and tight schedules, which resulted in large gangs working at a frenetic pace:

Unloading a 'spud boat'—' a human ant bed'.

To come on a wharf when a fruit boat or a spud boat was discharging was like coming upon a human ant bed. Speed of discharge was sought, and there was only one way to give it—put the men on and keep them going. To sort and stack these cargoes was like sorting a bucket of hundreds and thousands. The fruit and spud boat manifests would contain anything up to five hundred separate marks, and these, coming higgledy-piggledy out of the ship had to be stacked in their own separate locations.[62]

Local fortunes rose and fell in response to the rhythms of the shipping industry, and to the patterns of activity set in motion by international trade requirements. In general terms, Australia's heavy reliance on trade in primary produce made it peculiarly vulnerable to external events, but the enormous upheavals of World War I, followed by the trade boom of the twenties and the economic collapse of the thirties, were felt immediately and powerfully in a place like Millers Point. Local industries or workshops which might have responded to different rhythms had all but disappeared from the area by this time.

The range of employment provided by the port was vast. In addition to the men who worked the ships at sea, there were men who maintained, outfitted and provisioned them while in port. To the labours of the wharfie were added those of carters, and later lorrymen, and of the storemen and packers who worked in the warehouses and bond stores which

---

62 James Gaby, *The Restless Waterfront* (Antipodean, Sydney, 1974), p 18.

lined the streets behind the wharves. If this were a study of Sydney's maritime industries there would be a great complexity of occupations, trade unions, employers' associations and Government enquires with which to deal. But in a history of Millers Point, it is the wharf labourer who looms the largest in the twentieth century. Earlier, the distinctions between seamen and the various types of waterside workers were more blurred, in terms of work carried out, and in the early years of the century there may have been a few small outfits still using the same labour to unload and to man the ships. The dominant reality, however, was the increasing organisation of wharf labourers, who were beginning to come within the terms of the arbitration system and whose jobs were ever more clearly delineated. Within the social framework of Millers Point, as a rough rule of thumb, single men went to sea, but once married they looked for shore work. It was married men who were likely to get access to the Harbour Trust's houses, and to settle into the life of The Point. The seaman, who came and went, would be more likely to take a room on a casual basis, although many did maintain a permanent address in one of the big boarding houses which lined Lower Fort Street and dotted the rest of the district. These houses, formerly the mansions of the long-departed professional and merchant elite, were also owned by the Harbour Trust, but managed by landlords on a commercial basis.

In practice, the same individual might have been both seaman and wharfie in turn, and many of the male residents of Millers Point went to sea or were retired seamen. Indeed many of them were 'foreign' in the

Harold Greenhill: Waterfront Workers, 1946.

sense that they were not of the dominant Anglo-Celtic stock, so that the accents in the street in the early years of the century were as varied as the names—Jorgensen, Olsen, Isberg, Van Kampen and Wulf as well as Murray and Anderson, Hurley and McBride. Scandinavian and Germanic names became enmeshed in generations of Millers Pointers. The women whom these men married were likely to be of local stock with ties to the neighbourhood, so that acceptance was relatively easy. Local pride in the cosmopolitan community of the port was readily developed. In the 1920s when British immigration to Australia was high, the Church of England's Migration Council Office was located in the grounds of the Garrison Church and many services of welcome for migrants were held there.[63]

But not withstanding this general tolerance of cultural diversity, outsiders could be stigmatised to deflect criticism away from the Millers Point community. By emphasising

---

63 A.W. Morton, *The History of the Garrison Church*, p 12.

the 'otherness' of seamen when it suited them, the locals had a ready-made explanation for the unsavoury reputation attributed to Miller Point by many residents of Sydney at large. While they believed that the streets of Millers Point were dangerous and the social ways sordid, locals remember it as a close supportive community, where doors need never be locked, and where 'Mum herself and old Mrs Merriman who lived next door and old Mrs Sainty who lived across the road, they could sit here of a hot night, on their chairs, and have a good talk'. In remembering these things, Mr McBride, who was born in Agar Street in 1903, explained the reputation for danger by reference to an 'external' element:

> *We had a lot of shipping around here and you didn't know who'd come to the shore with the ship. They'd come ashore amongst themselves. They'd have a few of our beers, which was too heavy for them. They'd be fighting amongst themselves, Millers Point got the blame for that . . . we'd talk to them, but being silly with the drink, they wanted to fight. Well, you had to protect yourself.*[64]

One group that Pointers always distanced themselves from was the Chinese, who lived not in their community, but in The Rocks. The proximity of numbers of citizens of Chinese descent just beyond the Argyle Cut meant that locals contributed their share of bigotry towards this group, which was a ready target during the plague scare and at other times of stress. But this form of racism was endemic in Sydney, and went unnoticed amid the claims for community. And despite the remembered neighbourliness, there can be no doubt that among the wharf-labouring population itself, in the days prior to World War II, there was much division, acrimony and bitterness, generated by a powerful shipping industry which always sought to arrange labouring work in ways calculated to divide and demoralise the workforce.

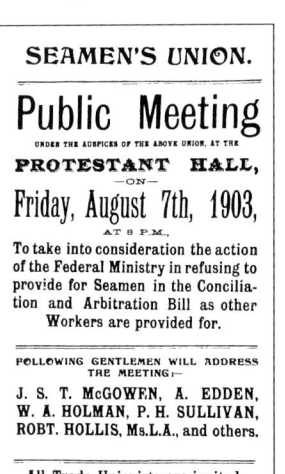

The reformed Sydney Wharf Labourers Union which had been established in 1899, formed the nucleus of the Waterside Workers Federation (WWF) in 1902. Under the leadership of secretary, W.M. (Billy) Hughes, local member for West Sydney and later Prime Minister of Australia, the union made various gains from the new arbitration system, including recognition of preference for unionists in 1902, and eventually the first national award for casual workers, handed down by Justice Higgins in 1914.[65] Conditions continued to be primitive, and the work exhausting, but in comparison with the strikes, drought and depression of the 1890s, things were a little less grim, work more plentiful and the waterfront was relatively peaceful until the war.

But with the war came increased living costs and reduced jobs. In July 1917 a strike at the tramways workshops in Randwick rapidly developed into a general strike which included seamen and waterside workers, who were out for ten weeks. The Government was swift to

---

64 McBride in Trish FitzSimons, '*The Point's Changed* . . . , p 17.
65 Winifred Mitchell, 'Sydney's Wharfies', in Garry Wotherspoon, *Sydney's Transport*, pp 28–31.

In class 6B, Fort Street School, 1919, the children were of varied ethnic stock.

use the fact of wartime conditions to accuse the strikers of national disloyalty, and promised that unionists who helped break the strike could be assured of continued union membership and preference under new union banners if need be, when the strike was defeated. 'Loyalists', or 'scabs', depending on your point of view, were ready to work the ships, and were conducted to work under police protection. They were housed in various localities around the harbour including the five storey building in Kent Street, Millers Point, which had operated since 1882 as the 'Model Lodging House', providing accommodation for single men. In 1902 the Sydney Harbour Trust took control of the building, which it continued to run as a lodging house, and by making it available to 'loyalists'/'scabs', the Government was providing amenities for this group which far exceeded any so far provided for other workers. The new and improved wharves which the Trust had built for the ship owners to rent, contained no water taps, shelters or toilets for the labourers, and union attempts to gain even these basic amenities were fought against long and hard by the ship owners. In 1917 there could be no doubt whose side the Government was on, while the dissension between men generated an intensity of ill feeling long to be remembered. Much of the bitterness arose from the fact that it was Prime Minister Billy Hughes who was leading the attack on the Union. In the 1980s, Mr McBride recalled:

> Dad had his strike, the 1917 strike, the big strike, when all the coalies went out to support other unions, which then come down scabs on them. That was the 1917 strike. The Railway and Tramway Struggle caused the strike but then other unions went out in sympathy with them. But them men in the railway and trams come down scabbing on them on the waterfront. It led to trouble.[66]

---

66 McBride in Trish FitzSimons, *The Point's Changed . . .*, p 13.

1917. The wharfies were on strike but there were plenty of others who 'came down scabs on them'.

His father was not prepared to ride public transport operated by strikebreakers, even when he had to walk from Millers Point to Botany to work, 'he was that solid like all the rest of them union members was'.

But they were not all solid, and what unity there had been was in tatters. In place of preference for employment of men wearing the union medal, there were now three pick-up bureaus, two controlled by the ship owners, one by the Government. The role of these bureaus is discussed by Tom Nelson, a trade union organiser in the thirties, in his history of the union, *The Hungry Mile*.

According to Nelson, the bureau which supplied men for the Darling Harbour-based interstate ships was open to WWF members who possessed an employer's metal disc. Charges of corruption in obtaining discs were inevitable, while the employers' habit of always allocating jobs in numerical order of the numbered discs ensured work for the 'early birders'—those who had broken ranks from the strike to register early. Those with high numbers got little work and had time to organise for a fairer system. Many WWF members were unable to obtain a disc at all, and could only get work at the dock gates in busy times.

The second bureau was located in what Nelson called 'Vinegar Lane', Millers Point (probably near Towns's Wharf), and contained the 'loyalists'/'scabs'. These men formed the Permanent and Casual Wharf Labourers Union and some were paid weekly wages. They were hired out to the overseas stevedoring companies, and shared the deep sea work with the members of the third bureau, housed in the old Coal Lumpers Hall, now the Abraham Mott Hall, in Argyle Place. Here, returned soldiers were given numbered discs, and employed in the same way as the Sussex Street men. The Government's Preference for Returned Soldiers Act, which applied to all industries, rankled in some quarters, but in the case of the wharf labourers, resentment was made more complex by the practice of giving returned soldiers who were also WWF members high disc numbers and little work.[67]

The strength of the ship owners' victory was clearly evidenced in these new hiring arrangements, which generated many ugly scenes and angry run-ins between labourers in the years following 1917. But the sheer brutality of the system also continued to outrage the WWF and the waterfront was worked under an uneasy truce, with constant threats of renewed strike action. By the early twenties, with work becoming more plentiful, the WWF regained control. Though it had not supported a major strike of seamen in 1919, the increased wages and better conditions which resulted from the seamen's resounding victory over the ship owners cannot have harmed the Unionists' resolve to end the conditions they were working under.[68]

A system of vigilance officers began to police regulations and award conditions, a practice which became crucial in reducing victimisation and enforcing officially sanctioned, but often flouted, conditions. Barney Mullins, who was one of the first vigilance officers, and subsequently a member of parliament, is usually mentioned in relation to achieving the closure of the hated bureaus and the ending of the disc system in 1924. By then, black bans on cargoes and threats of strikes signalled renewed union strength.[69]

But that was just one battle in an ongoing war. Ship owners were constantly interested in asserting voluntary or licensing systems above union-based registration, and arbitration over industrial action. In 1928 the notorious Transport Workers Act reintroduced the notion of licences, and work was declared open to anyone who purchased a transport worker's licence. This so-called 'Dog Collar Act' was not successful in Sydney where work was plentiful and where the WWF, which had so recently managed to oust a similar system, managed to hold on to preference for its members.[70] But as prosperity turned into depression at the end of the decade, conditions deteriorated anyway, and jobs disappeared. James Gaby, who arrived on the waterfront in 1922 and became a foreman stevedore, recalled that he might pick up forty labourers from a crowd of three or four hundred 'hungry, desperate men':

> They'd go to the Millers Point pick up at 8 o'clock. There were hundreds of men down at Central Wharf—8 and 9 wharves—The bloke would come out and he'd get on the box and say 'you, you, you and you'. They were bloody hard times. If they never got a job, they'd have to get to Pyrmont for the next pick up. They'd run, or run-walk. You

---

67 Tom Nelson, *The Hungry Mile* (Newsletter Printery, Sydney, 1951), pp 66–68.
68 Richard Morris, 'The 1919 Seamen's Strike', *Labour History*, No 37 (November 1979), pp 52–62. For a general history of the Seamen's Union see B. Fitzpatrick and R.J. Cahill, *The Seamen's Union of Australia 1872–1972* (Sydney, Seamen's Union, 1981).
69 James Gaby, *The Restless Waterfront*, pp 9–12.
70 Richard Morris, 'Australian Stevedoring and Shipping Labour under the Transport Workers Act 1928-47', *Great Circle*, Vol 11, No 2 (1989), pp 17–27.

couldn't run all the way. Then if they missed that one, they'd walk over to Woolloomooloo. Things were destitute.[71]

In 1935, with thousands still out of work on the waterfront, but with the worst of it over for shippers, a strike of seamen over the issue of payment for deferred sailing time spread throughout the industry, eventually resulting in complete defeat for the Seamens' Union, which won none of its claims and suffered set backs in conditions. Sydney was made a 'prescribed port' for merchant shipping under the Transport Workers Act, which meant that seamen had to have a licence, and there was no shortage of men willing to apply for them. By mid-1936 there were three licensed seamen for every job available, as well as volunteer bureaus, this time for sailors, and the Seamen's Union was in disarray.[72] The wharf labourers did not support the seamen in this strike, but the lessons learned from the endless cycles of improved conditions followed by repression and disintegration—clearly in evidence across the waterfront in the twenties and thirties—were important in hardening class attitudes and extending radical politics.

In 1930 a Communist Branch of the WWF was formed, and many believed that its energies prevented total collapse of morale in the grim years of that decade. Regardless of its industrial fortunes, the Union sustained many workers in varied ways. Some found its involvement in international struggles exciting and educational. 'The wharves were my education, and the Spanish Civil War my first political lesson,' recalled one labourer who began his wharf work in the Depression.[73] For others, the sustaining role of the Union in cases of individual hardship was a great security. The Union would 'get up a benefit', pay for a funeral, take up a collection at the gate—charity which was easy to accept because 'they didn't do it to one, they did it to everybody'.[74]

The increasing success of the Union in gaining real improvements to conditions was beginning to be seen by the end of the thirties, but its coincidence with the ending of the Depression and the outbreak of World War II makes it more of a story for later on.

When wharf labourers were not operating under the bureau system, they were employed by the traditional methods of selection by stevedore's agents at various pick-up points. This system of hiring maintained the 'bull system', whereby the ablest and strongest got the most work. Ship owners and stevedores were obviously in favour of employing the best and most tractable workers, while the 'bulls' themselves worked to maintain the power of their own gang against the strength of the Union for their own immediate personal gain. From 1913 the Union attempted to restrict the number of consecutive hours of work to 28, but without success. It was not uncommon for men to work twice that many hours if the opportunity presented itself, with cases of up to eighty

---

71 James Gaby, *The Restless Waterfront*, p 28; Interview with Thomas Callaghan, Leichhardt, 1991.
72 L.J. Louis, 'Recovery from the Depression and the Seamen's Strike, 1935–36', *Labour History*, No 41 (November 1981), pp 74–86.
73 Conversations with retired workers at WWF, Sydney Branch, Sussex Street, 1987. See Rupert Lockwood, *War on the Waterfront: Menzies, Japan and the Pig-iron Dispute* (Hale & Iremonger, Sydney, 1987) for an account of the most famous 'action' of this period.
74 Helena Goss in Trish FitzSimons, '*The Point's Changed* . . . , p 51.

six hours being recorded.[75] Personal gain in the short term resulted in 'bulls' being unconcerned to limit excessive weights of loads, and their pace of working became the measure for all the others. Their earnings were correspondingly greater than for other labourers on the waterfront, and machismo models of masculinity, while deeply resented, were also deeply admired.

Millers Point residents were quick to make heroes of local pugilists for similar reasons. When Hughie MacIntosh, 'a big lump of a man . . . rangy and muscular', arrived in town there was 'a natural niche for him—the bull gangs at Dals wheat and wool, this gang made the pace, and you had to be one hundred per cent man to stay with it. Big Joe Beckett, an ex-heavyweight fighter, was boss'.[76]

Inevitably, wharf work under these conditions resulted in sickness, deformity and sometimes death. Lumping bagged wheat for a season might set up the labourer and his family for months to come, but after a few seasons, he was likely to be physically less able. After years of such labour, his ribs might overlap.[77] Constant use of the hook to move bales of wool could result in permanent clawing of the hand, while handling of cargoes like loose asbestos could be lethal. Dr Roland McQueen examined forty to sixty year old men

Coalies at work. Opinion is divided over what constituted the worst cargo to handle, but according to Harry Ball, it was lampblack. 'You'd come home and scrub yourself clean, but by morning your skin would be black again. It would come through the pores'.

---

75 Tom Nelson, *The Hungry Mile*, p 59.
76 James Gaby, *The Restless Waterfront*, p 50.
77 Winifred Mitchell, 'Sydney's Wharfies', p 35.

for an inquiry into the industry in 1943, and found a wide range of illnesses and deformities. He claimed to have worked with shearers and timber workers, but 'neither of these industries can produce any comparable number of physical derelicts as I have encountered amongst the waterside workers of Sydney'. His assessment of the Depression years was of a 'devastating toll' on 'men who in the main had been ruined physically'.[78]

But it was more than just the sacrifice of the men's health which was required to keep the industry going, and though much has been written about the labour of such men, less has been recorded about the unpaid labour of family members which was required to support them. Everyone in Millers Point worked, though most were not paid for it, and labourers who had the support of wives or mothers were more likely to make a go of it than those without. Often the children too were involved in the task of keeping the wharf labourer fed and able to work. About the time of World War I, Elsie Olsen (née Solomon) recalled that her father, a coal lumper, often worked at Balls Head 'for a couple of days or three days at a time and you'd have to pack up all their meals and send them over to them, so they'd have something to eat. My sister used to take them over.' Molly Connaghan remembered the same kind of trip to Pyrmont:

> *You'd have two plates, enamel plates; an old plate on top wrapped up in a serviette. His soup and his dinner would be in that. We used to take it to wherever they were working so they'd have a hot meal, because they'd work twenty four hours.*[79]

These operations were complicated and time consuming, but other contributions, like being skilled at dealing with accidents and sickness, were far more demanding. Vera McDonald remembers her mother tending the neighbours when they were sick, or laying out the dead, and these memories are shared by many women who grew up in the first three decades of the twentieth century. 'Granny' Goss was often not at home for her own family in the morning, because she'd been called out to a neighbour's during the night:

> *She'd help, whatever would happen with them. Perhaps they just wanted nursing, they might have wanted bathing and things like that. She'd give them their medicine or anything like that. She wasn't paid. That was just neighbourly.*[80]

It was also skilled work, which helped the community to survive. Doctors were rarely called for, and children were born in the U.S.F.R.—upstairs in the front room—with the assistance of a midwife. Early in the century it might have been Mrs Ellis in Argyle Place or Ann Williams from Kent Street, later Nurse Martin, who lived in Lower Fort Street, still fondly remembered by many older residents, near the century's end.

Children contributed to the domestic economy by involvement in the complex network of childminding and tending the elderly, which inevitably evolved in this close-knit neighbourhood where several generations often lived in the same house. Many remember

---

78 Report of Ronald McQueen to Commonwealth Stevedoring Industry Commission, 1943, cited in Tom Nelson, *The Hungry Mile*, pp 115–18.
79 Molly Connaghan in Trish FitzSimons, '*The Point's Changed . . .*, pp 21, 61.
80 Ibid, p 50.

St Michael's, Lower Fort Street in 1923. This building, used as a religious residence and an orphanage, was demolished for the Bridge.

their days spent at St Brigid's, or St Patrick's, or maybe at Fort Street High, being punctuated by the need to fetch and carry, or to tend to a multitude of chores, while the irregularity of hours of labouring work made it almost impossible for family members to maintain commitments or social activities on a regular basis. This was especially true for wives.[81]

Coping in lean times through the sharing of food, clothing and money operated both informally, through neighbourhood networks, and formally, through the friendly society work of the unions. It was also practised in relation to the religious who taught at St Brigid's in Kent Street. According to Mrs Farrer, whose parents ran a barber's shop in the cluster of shops across the road, if the shopkeepers had not taken the nuns their dinners, they would have been 'very very hungry'. Others recall bringing food for them from the convent at St Patrick's. When the Little Sisters of the Poor visited the area to collect offerings in kind from the local traders, Mrs Farrer's mother often gave them a ten shilling note to buy stationery at the paper shop, because 'she couldn't give them a haircut or a shave, could she?'[82] In these ways the

Father Piquet is best remembered for being generous of spirit and charming. He worked in the area from the 1880s to the 1930s.

81 Margaret Adamson, 'Networks', in Kate Blackmore and Paul Ashton, *Parallax: The Rocks* (Arcadia Press, Sydney, 1987).
82 Farrer in Trish FitzSimons, '*The Point's Changed* . . . , p 88; Mary Musgrave in 'Point People'.

social practices of the community of The Point were reinforced by official church practice.

Yet, despite this kind of unpaid support, the primary wage earners often did not make enough to maintain a family, and though there were occasional times of plenty, lean times were far more common. Lillian Smith born in 60 High Street in 1912 used to go office cleaning with her mother when she was twelve. 'We used to set out at 4.30a.m. to walk along Hickson Street to scrub bare boards for the Maritime Services Board.'[83] In the worst times, outside help had to be resorted to. During the 1917 strike, 'we used to get a handout, around near Motts Hall (Coal Lumpers Union). People, some firms too, would leave food parcels there. You never had the dole then'.[84] In the Depression, when the dole was introduced, it was in kind, with coupons redeemable at grocery shops like Downton and Dyer, in George Street North. On more permanent standby was the Benevolent Society, which gave food to approved recipients at its offices near Central Railway, and during the Depression sent a used-clothes wagon into needy areas like Millers Point.[85]

In less depressed times it was often only the supplementary earning of other family members that kept the household together. Though the idea of married women 'working' was unacceptable, and simply not practical when husbands and sons had to be supported in their wharf work, in times of strike or prolonged unemployment of the men, women often did work at whatever casual jobs they could outside the home. On a more permanent basis, incomes were supplemented by doing laundry work and taking paying lodgers. With no shower facilities provided for workers on the wharves, 'coalies used to pay Mrs Smith in Argyle Street and a few others something like ten shillings a week to wash before going home'.[86]

Children contributed to the domestic economy by collecting firewood for the stove, and selling it by the barrow load to housewives; and the watchmen on the wharves employed to guard against pilfering were often amenable to letting kids they recognised take odd bits of timber. Many outsiders believed that survival through 'lifting' goods in the course of wharf work was common. This was perceived as a problem immediately following World War I and in 1922 a conference of concerned parties decided that the formation of a special twenty four man Harbour Police Force was necessary. However, improved private policing of the wharves, perhaps inspired by the realisation that they would have to contribute financially to such a force, resulted in the shippers reporting minimal pillage by 1923, and the idea was dropped. In 1931, a depression year when things were very grim in many wharfside households, the Trust reported that pilfering was low, perhaps at the 'irreductible minimum'. On the other hand, there were exceptions. When World War II was declared and enemy ships were given twenty four hours to leave the harbour, locals, in an upsurge of patriotic fervour 'went on a rampage and knocked off a lot of o.p. rum that night'.[87]

---

83 Lillian Smith, in *Point People*.
84 Trish FitzSimons, 'The Point's Changed . . . , p 13.
85 Personal Communication, Thomas Callaghan, Leichhardt, 1990.
86 Personal Communication, Vera McDonald, Kent Street, 1990.
87 SHT, *AR* 1923, pp 2–4; Personal Communication, Joyce Phillips, Kent Street, 1990.

Then there was fishing. This undoubtedly contributed to the maintenance of many families, though few thought of it as work. Patrick Callaghan recalled that:

> A young lad could have a lot of fun fishing from the wharves and at the same time supply some extra food for the family. Pocket money could be made by catching 'yellowtail' and selling them as bait at twelve for three pence . . . during the season tailor were often caught in large numbers and when they were running the wharf would be packed with locals fishing for good cheap food.[88]

For some it was a serious business, like Norm White, who took to fishing after a neck injury sustained while lumping coal left him unable to do heavy work and without compensations. So he fished, perhaps catching three or four jewfish, one for his tea and the others to raffle in the pubs in the evening.[89]

For others fishing was play, devised with all the creativity and resourcefulness that, at its best, a poor community will generate. Cecil Henry remembers a childhood which included going fishing in boats made from packing cases found on the wharves. The cracks in the cases would be sealed with tar from the Council's tar dumps, and a piece of 'one be one', split at the end into two shafts, each with a bent nail wired on, served as weapons to spear the fish.

The physical barrier of the Bridge reinforced the reality of the village of Millers Point.

---

88 Personal Communication, Patrick Callaghan, St Ives, 1990.
89 Personal Communication, Joyce Phillips, Kent Street, 1990.

By World War II the people of Millers Point formed a more close-knit community than any other in Sydney. The glare of publicity which had engulfed the area at the turn of the century had left in its wake a community of workers and families tied to the wharves and the port through work and by the residential advantages to be gained from the Sydney Harbour Trust, which since 1936 had been reconstituted as the Maritime Services Board. Access to houses was through involvement in local work or because of membership of a family already resident in the area, and by now second and third generation families were on the books of 'The Maritime', quite apart from those whose links with the area stretched back into the previous century. These housing preferences reinforced the trend towards a narrower range of jobs. Many men in particular rarely left the area of the wharves with their attendant stores and public houses, and while other work and some entertainment was sought in nearby business areas of the city, close family and neighbourhood networks meant that much of the residents' social life was also conducted locally. This was reinforced by lack of surplus spending power and by irregular hours of work.

The Sydney Harbour Bridge, completed in 1932, had reinforced the physical barrier of the natural ridge between Millers Point and The Rocks, while the widespread preference for suburban living which the Bridge symbolised made places like Millers Point ever more ignored by Sydneysiders at large. The village was more inward looking and more differentiated from the rest of Sydney than at any other time since convicts began to create the Argyle Cut.

Millers Point in 1937. The big building in the foreground is Dalgety's Store. The recently completed Sydney Harbour Bridge dominates the Harbour behind.

4

FROM 1939 TO THE PRESENT

On the eve of World War II there were signs that the Depression was over in Millers Point, though this was not to say that conditions were good. The tonnage of shipping had been steadily increasing for several years, and the numbers of men employed directly by the Maritime Services Board had increased from a low of 360 in 1934 to 580 by 1938, but there were still many unemployed.[1] In that year, the Board contributed materially to the water carnival on the harbour to mark the 150th anniversary of white settlement in Sydney, but had not yet provided water taps for labourers on the wharves, and the struggling parish of the Garrison Church was so short of cash that it decided to use its longstanding church tower fund to repair the leaking roof.[2]

But if the years immediately preceding the war seemed unremarkable at the time, with hindsight they would be recalled by many as the beginning of real changes on the waterfront, and hence in the adjoining households. The changes are closely associated with the name of Jim Healy, the Communist union organiser, who became general secretary of the Waterside Workers Federation in October 1937, and presided over massive changes in conditions on the waterfront during the war years. 'Big Jim' is recalled by many workers with something akin to adulation and in their eyes, there was nothing Healy could not do: 'I've seen him take on the greatest barristers in this country . . . I heard Calwell say that if he'd stayed in the Labor Party he would have been Prime Minister'.[3] Less partisan observers point out that, although he carried the vote in the Union, this never translated into a large scale defection from traditional support for the Labor Party at general elections, and while he undoubtedly had considerable powers to unite and hold the men through numerous strikes and industrial campaigns, success was assisted by conditions of the war, which provided an environment conducive to accommodating union demands.

Jim Healy, General Secretary of the Waterside Workers Federation, 1937–61.

Shipping increased during, and because of, the war, with large amounts of military personnel and equipment passing through the port, especially after Japan entered the conflict. Urgent need to maintain order and achieve rapid turnaround on the waterfront led to the creation of a Stevedoring Industry

---

1 MSB, *AR* 1938, p 13.
2 A.W. Morton, *The History of the Garrison Church*, p 13.
3 Conversations with retired workers at WWF, Sydney Branch, Sussex Street, 1987; Victor Williams, *The Years of Big Jim* (Lone Hand Press, Perth, 1975).

Commission and a Maritime Industry Commission in 1942. With emphasis on efficiency, rather than the more traditional support for shippers, a situation was created where demands of strong unions were often achieved in exchange for general cooperation.[4]

The most significant change to working conditions came with the introduction of the gang rotary system of hiring wharf labour, in 1943, after sixteen days of strikes and wild mass meetings. The ending of the bull system and the establishment of rotating rosters for hiring registered workers resulted in the even distribution of work, and increased unity between workers who had previously viewed each other as rivals for scarce jobs or, when jobs were plentiful, as they were during the war, had jostled for the most favoured jobs. Examples had included the most experienced men choosing night work, which was better paid, leaving day shifts to snipers (unskilled, non-union men); and avoiding unpopular cargoes, like double-dumped wool, which reduced volume and increased weight, enabling two ships to carry the normal load of three, 'for the war effort'.

Initially, the roster system created some stress, as bulls lost their positions of power, and old scores had to be evened out between labourers with past grievances, but the long term effect was a united front, and by 1950 the snipers and the old employer-created Permanent and Casual Union had been absorbed by the WWF. Labourers were no longer dependent on the whims of the stevedores, and according to James Gaby, men no longer joked with the foremen. Such joking would have been motivated by a need to curry favour. Under the new regime the men were a little more free to acknowledge their actual relationship with the foreman—that 'they hated the pannos from Millers Point'.

Panno, as a title for an overseer or minor official probably comes from 'tinpot'—i.e. pannikin, but some wharfies reckoned it doubly suitable, because 'they were panickin' you all the time'. As an overseer, Gaby believed that the rate of work was slower than in the pre-roster days. Many would have agreed, but they would have added 'thank God'. The new system was, he admitted, 'a great leveller'.[5]

Gaby, who had long been a stevedore, was now the employers' delegate on the newly formed Board of Reference, along with a representative of the Federal Government and of the Union. The Board's job, which was to inspect and deliberate on disputes over work practices as they arose on the waterfront, was indicative of the trend towards cooperation between a strong union of men and ship owners who had grown used to Government control.

The Stevedoring Industry Commission was maintained on a more permanent basis after the war, and in a booming economy, conditions improved for the workforce. Two shifts in 24 hours, some annual leave and finally sick pay and an allowance on days when work was unavailable did not bring them into line with many other industries, but compared to pre-war conditions, things were vastly improved. Canteens were set up at out-of-the-way wharves, washing facilities were established, special buses ran from the wheat wharves at Glebe Island back into town at the changeover in shift at 9p.m. and pay was obtained through a central office. This latter concession indicated a profound shift in

---
4 Richard Morris, 'Australian Stevedoring and Shipping Labour . . . 1928–47'. *Great Circle*, Vol 11, No 2, 1989, pp 25–27.
5 James Gaby, *The Restless Waterfront*, pp 214–15.

Front row, left to right: Harry (Snowy) Teasel, Stan Moran, Ray Jones, Ron Maxwell, during a campaign in 1956.

relationships. It put to an end the ignominious rushing from wharf to wharf at the end of the week to collect bits and pieces of pay, or worse, sending the children, as Molly Connaghan recalled of earlier times when 'if my father was working I used to have to go down and collect his money on a Saturday morning'.[6] None of these conditions was achieved without industrial action, and the waterfront quickly gained a reputation in some quarters for being provocatively confrontationalist. But for the men involved, if that is what it was going to take to obtain even simple things like pegs to hang their coats on, then that was what they would do.

An intense struggle occurred again in 1954 with shippers attempting to regain control of the hiring system, but they were unsuccessful, and it was not till late in the twentieth century that deregulation of the industry re-emerged as an issue.

The backdrop to these changes was post-war economic expansion, with the MSB reporting in 1950 that ships were waiting off shore for berths and that turnaround time was slow, due to labour shortages and stoppages.[7] With full employment right through to the early seventies, wharf work now generated secure jobs.

---

6 Molly Connaghan in Trish FitzSimons, *'The Point's Changed . . .'*, p 20.
7 MSB, *AR* 1950–51, pp 16, 17.

Cargo in Hickson Road, 1950s.

But if the conditions of work changed rapidly in the wake of the war, the built fabric of Millers Point and its wharves did not. There was no pressure to alter or extend the wharves for two reasons. The shift away from shipping to land transport on coastal runs continued; and the trend towards smaller numbers of ships meant that, even with increased tonnage, undue strain was not placed on wharfage, while the earlier practice of leasing out wharves to private companies was gradually replaced by state control after the establishment of the MSB in 1936, allowing more rational use of facilities.[9]

Neither was there pressure to alter the housing stock of Millers Point. A general housing shortage during the Depression and the austerity years of the war no doubt resulted in 'doubling up' of families as it did for Helen Klapdor. She married her serviceman husband in 1941 in Trinity Church 'one Saturday night'. They celebrated the event at her mother's place around the pianola, then went to her new home, at her husband's house at 42 Windmill Street, where she spent Sunday settling in before going to work on Monday.

> *My father-in-law lived with us. We shared everything downstairs. Then upstairs, when we first got married, we had another uncle living there. He had a back room and then my father-in-law had the middle room, and we had the biggest room, the balcony room. I had a double bed in there, and I had one baby in the cot and my son in a single*

---

8 MSB, *AR* 1950–51, pp 15.
9 Peter Proudfoot, 'The Extension of Maritime Activity in Sydney . . . 1890–1950', *Great Circle*, Vol 10, No 2, 1988, pp 112–14.

bed. Then when I was going to have another baby, I had to put the big boy [somewhere], we made a room for him out on the verandah, had it half closed in. Then we got rid of the uncle, and my father-in-law took over the back room and we had the middle room for the boy and the girl.[10]

This kind of overcrowding was widespread in Sydney in the wake of the Depression and World War II, but the twentieth century preference for suburban living was stronger than ever after the war, and housing such as Millers Point had to offer was increasingly rejected.

When the MSB was first established in 1936 it suggested to the Government that some other organisation take over the administration of its housing and retail properties, but nothing came of this.[11] The Government had no structures in place to administer public housing since the demise of the Housing Board in the twenties, and the City Council, once anxious to gain control of the area, now showed no interest in it. After the war, the issue of public housing was definitely on the political agenda, but Millers Point was not. Financial considerations resulted in the newly created Housing Commission building in industrial areas and in outer suburbs, and paying very little attention to the inner, decaying core of the city. And so things went on much as usual in Millers Point. The practice of renting property to local workers and local families did not conform to any rational criteria for providing state housing for those most in need, but it created a cohesive community which generated minimal administrative problems for the Board. Basic repair to buildings were carried out by the MSB when required, while surveillance over internal alterations was minimal and the tenants were allowed maximum freedom to do their own 'improvements'. Undoubtedly many of the terraces grew longer as extensions went on the back of the houses to accommodate large families. In general, this lack of interference contributed to a sense of de facto ownership, although in Helen Klapdor's case, it may have contributed to a sense of frustration. When she moved into the Windmill Street house in 1941 it was lit by gas downstairs and candles upstairs, because her husband's grandmother 'didn't believe in electricity'. Similarly, many of the residents did not believe in spending money on the kinds of kitchen and bathroom amenities which were rapidly becoming standard elsewhere in Sydney, but which were not obligatory in Millers Point. But while the MSB's low level of intervention may not have been the best policy for maintaining the fabric of the houses, it possibly contributed to the general wellbeing of the community which was left free to pursue its own social ways. 'As long as you kept your fronts clean your were right with the Maritime,' according to Vera McDonald, who recalled that everyone used to hose down their front steps and the adjoining public footpath regularly out of a sense of caring for property which may not have been theirs, but was definitely assumed to be secure, not only for their own use, but for their children and descendents. Consequently, a degree of internal policing occurred, while 'The Maritime', as paternal landlord, would send a representative to local funerals, and minimised grievances by providing ready access to residents at its offices at Circular Quay.[12]

---

10 Helen Klapdor in Trish FitzSimons, '*The Point's Changed . . .* , p 82.
11 MSB, *AR* 1936, p 18.
12 Personal Communication, Vera McDonald, Kent Street, 1990.

The one group of residents who may not have felt secure were the people who lived in the large 'residentials', previously the grand houses of the merchants and sea captains of the nineteenth century which lined Lower Fort Street, and parts of Kent Street, Merriman Street and Dalgety Terrace. Since the takeover by the Harbour Trust, these houses were on long term leases to 'head tenants', who paid a rent for the house, but were free to let the rooms to whomever they chose. The head tenants sold or passed on leases at will, and although none of the property was owned by them, they were always known as landlords or landladies. The rents of the head tenants were low, on the understanding that they would personally maintain the properties, but again there was little surveillance by the port authority, and because they were not licensed as boarding houses they were operated free of constraints which applied to many similar houses in the city. Once again these arrangements minimised the involvement of the MSB and provided scope for the head tenants to neglect the houses. They also failed to provide security for the occupants who could be evicted at the head tenant's whim. On the other hand, this too established a level of internal policing which maintained a neighbourhood cohesion. Rooms were let out to transients and new arrivals to the country, but also to seamen who might keep on a room permanently so that they had a familiar base in port, or, like 'old Bill Gallager, would know how to arrive just as a room came empty'. For others, like old Mrs O'Brien, it was home. She and her wharfie husband moved into a 'bed-sit' with a small kitchen in Lower Fort Street in the 1930s and there she died in 1989.

Many of the residentials provided rooms, but not cooking facilities. While most Sydneysiders did the 'Australian' thing of breakfasting in the privacy of their home, the wharf areas followed what was considered to be European practice, and breakfast might be had at several little restaurants in Kent Street, or at the 'Busy Bee' or the 'Centenary Cafe' in Lower George Street, over on The Rocks.[13]

Some of the best information on the kinds of people who lived in Millers Point is contained in the city electoral rolls for Gipps Ward.[14] The list for 1947 is the first one compiled under legislation which based voting eligibility on an adult sufferage, so that everyone who was eligible to vote on the state roll was now also eligible to vote at local elections; therefore the new list theoretically contained the names of all occupiers over twenty one years of age. There were other categories of voters as well, but not in the Millers Point streets of the ward. Here there were no owners of property who lived elsewhere, nor shopkeepers who came in for the day and retreated to the suburbs in the evenings, but simply 'occupiers'. The exceptions to this were the William David MacDonalds, senior and junior, blacksmiths of Petersham, who for many years operated a forge in a tiny workshop built into the cliff face on MSB property in the narrow Roden's Lane behind Dalgety Terrace. For the rest, it was 'residence' which got them on the roll, and, from the government astronomer on Observatory Hill to the lowliest labourer, they owned none of it between them.

---

13 Personal Communication, Shirley Ball, Lower Fort Street, 1990.
14 NSCA CRS 53/40.

Community ties were strong and home entertainment common.

The roll records 655 adult women and 926 men living in Millers Point, an imbalance in favour of men which was compatible with the maritime functions of the area. As the list missed out all of the workers under twenty one years, it undercounts the resident workforce considerably, as most children would not have stayed on beyond the required minimum school-leaving age of fourteen. Nevertheless it is a useful guide to the occupations of those who lived in Millers Point at mid-century. This is not the same thing as the workforce, because many of the men who thronged the wharves and filled the pubs lived elsewhere. Rather, it is a measure of the permanent community. The roll tells us less about the women than the men, as fully 543 of the 655 said they were employed in 'home duties'. This label covered a multitude of actual tasks, and included much work which, if it were paid for, would be taken to contribute substantially to the national accounts. There is little point in going over the labours done by women outlined in the previous chapter, but it might be suggested that these figures point to the possibility of traditional roles for women lasting longer in Millers Point than in other parts of the city. In part, this could have been due to the relative lack of convenient factories and workplaces, but it was more probably linked to the ongoing demands of men with labouring jobs on irregular schedules.

Of the 113 women over twenty one who did work outside the home, most would have been unmarried daughters or spinsters, and it would seem that the nearby commercial district of the city offered the best hopes of employment. A few had skilled jobs of the traditional kind in dressmaking or printing, and some achieved the status of clerical work, with one designating herself 'secretary', but most were in unskilled service positions like barmaid, factory hand or packer. None held a job which would have required the completion of senior schooling. Two brave souls appeared on the roll as 'stripper'. This probably meant that they worked in a tobacco factory separating leaves from stems, but then again it may not have meant that. In an area of the city close to docks it would go without saying that some women made a living by providing sexual services to men, and in a time of social dislocation such as is caused by war, the demand for this work would increase. But an electoral roll is not the place to find such people as 'Drunk Nursey', who ran a boarding house—and more—in Merriman Street, and is remembered for often ending up in the gutter outside her house.[15] Residents in ordinary houses tended to blame the large residentials for catering to these trades, but the rolls also make it clear that these large houses were home for many families as well as for single people. This was the case until well into the sixties when the housing shortage in Sydney had eased.

For adult men, the largest occupational group was 'labourer', an ill-defined term in general, but within the context of the categories of work available in the area, many of them would have been associated with the wharves. Of the men's, 831 were able to be assigned a job category with a tolerable degree of certainty, and of these, 491 (fifty nine per cent) were labourers, seamen, wharf labourers, coal lumpers or pursued other less frequently named occupations related to the maritime industries, from painters and dockers to marine cooks. A further seven per cent were storemen and packers or drivers who would have been associated with the stores and warehouses behind the wharves, and within the ranks of the skilled workers, about half were engaged in metal-based jobs. It cannot be known for certain where these engineers, boilermakers and the like actually worked, but the maritime industries and the workshops of the MSB would seem to be likely contenders. These groups together accounted for seventy three per cent of the male occupations.

For the rest, there was a range of unskilled jobs like caretaker and watchman, which may have been local, or railway and factory work which were not. A small service group of shopkeepers, restauranters and publicans provided for daily needs, but there were no outlets for major consumer goods. A mere thirty seven people were engaged in professional, semi-professional or managerial jobs, which included the aforementioned astronomer and a meteorologist at the Observatory, but also the local postmaster and a gentleman who styled himself as a 'missionary'. Only eighteen men, quite likely sons of households, held clerical positions.

The people of Millers Point maintained a strong sense of identity, reinforced by common economic interests, throughout the fifties and sixties. They had access to the cultural and entertainment facilities of the city, of course, but there were continuing close ties with the local area. The local Darling Harbour branch of the Labor Party could rely on the support of more than two hundred members and the annual Christmas Party, when all the children received a gift, was an institution more social than political. Candidates who delivered election speeches from the customary back of a truck parked outside the Post Office could rely on an amiable audience. Dan Minogue, longstanding Federal member, was often seen chatting to locals in the streets, while Harry Jensen, Lord Mayor of Sydney

---

15 Personal Communication, Joyce Phillips, Kent Street, 1990.

from 1957 to 1965 and, thereafter, the local state member until 1981, is remembered officially through the naming of the Harry Jensen Centre in Argyle Place (1959) where older residents could come for company and a midday meal. May Jackson, who has long been a volunteer worker for the Centre recalled what a difference the place made, especially to those living in residentials.[16]

The Harry Jensen Centre and the older Abraham Mott Hall next door provided a focal point for local functions and meetings, which could, if required, spill over onto the 'village green' in the middle of Argyle Place. Just occasionally Millers Point would witness events of pomp and circumstance, like a special service at the Garrison Church to commemorate some aspect of military history, but these were viewed not so much as part of the community, but as a foil for it. And when the wife of a certain governor of New South Wales would arrive at the most convenient polling booth to Government House, at the Baby Health Clinic in Millers Point, and refuse all but the blue how-to-vote card with a 'No, thank you, I intend to vote Liberal', no-one feared for the safety of the vote. In 1953, when the electorate of King recorded a sixty eight per cent vote for the Labor candidate (D. Clyne), the net level of support at the Millers Point booth was 89.9%. But in the next election of 1956, with more choice available, the vote in Millers Point for the Labor candidate (A. Sloss) fell to sixty four per cent, with 26.4% of the vote going to other left wing candidates.

Tony Bradford. 'Born bred and lived all his life on The Point.' Deputy Lord Mayor of Sydney (1963–64, 1983–84) and for many years Secretary of the local branch of the ALP.

Yet by the fifties, despite the tightness of the community, there were already warning signs of internal strain. Rising wages and secure work encouraged many Millers Point families to participate in the quest for a suburban home. Home ownership was rapidly becoming more attainable for more people than at any time in the past. The introduction of a radio call up on 2KY for work gangs, along with the arrival of the telephone as a common commodity and the explosion in private ownership of cars all helped to sever the links between port work and residence. The provision of trams and buses had permitted workers to commute, but the car was a far greater incentive to do so. Pressure on housing was reduced in Millers Point, and it would not be many years before a shift in the age structure would become apparent—with the Activity Centre busy, but school enrolments declining. Fort Street Primary, for instance, went from an average daily attendance of 272 in 1955 to a low of 153 in 1963. Thereafter it stabilised, falling away again in the 1970s, to reach forty eight pupils by 1975.[17]

By the 1960s, the city was experiencing a boom in construction, and the old sandstone buildings of last century were giving way to the new high rises in steel and glass. The

---

16 May Jackson in Trish FitzSimons, 'The Point's Changed . . . , p 72.
17 History Unit, NSW Dept. of Education.

preferred scenario of centralising commercial activity and removing residential activities to the suburbs had been going on for many decades, but now, with economic expansion more rapid than it had been since the 1920s, developers looked with glee at areas like Woolloomooloo and The Rocks. It would just be a matter of clearing away the last remaining old slums in such places and turning them over to high-earning, high rise development. Millers Point, hidden from sight behind the Bridge, looked nervously at The Rocks. Here an international design competition in 1963 had awarded the honours to a plan which had retained a place for residents—but in high rise apartments in a redevelopment which swept away the entire built fabric of the place.[18]

This plan came to nothing, but did generate public protest and alert residents to what they might expect in the future. When the Askin Government set up the Sydney Cove Redevelopment Authority (SCRA) in 1968 with plans for huge office towers and classy hotels, there were immediate protests from resident groups, and by the end of 1971, the Builders Labourers Federation (BLF) and the Federated Engine Drivers and Firemen's Association (FEDFA) had placed bans on work in The Rocks.[19] Green bans, as they came to be known, tied up millions of development dollars in Sydney in the early seventies, and have by now secured a place in the history books as a remarkable phase in social and environmental relations, with residents and workers banding together to thwart

Second class, Fort Street Primary School, 1941.

---

18 James Wallace Pty Ltd, 'The Redevelopment of the Rocks Area', 1964, quoted in Peter Spearritt and Christina de Marco, *Planning Sydney's Future* (Allen & Unwin, Sydney, 1988), p 98.
19 Zula Nittim, 'The Coalition of Resident Action Groups' in Jill Roe (ed.), *Twentieth Century Sydney* (Hale & Iremonger, Sydney, 1980), p 235.

development which residents found unacceptable. Many Millers Point residents became involved in these battles, learning the skills of confronting and communicating with outside organisations, and no doubt also becoming more aware of the kinds of pressures which might eventually be placed on Millers Point.

When the SCRA began to refer to Millers Point as the 'West Rocks' in their publications, and other planning authorities quickly followed suit, this not only raised the ire of the locals, but clarified for many the potential future direction of events. They fought successfully to have the name 'West Rocks' dropped, just as they would fight a few decades later to retain the name 'Millers Point' in Australia Post's postcode listing, and to get the advertised destination—'The Rocks'—off buses terminating at Millers Point.

The reaction against rapid high density development in The Rocks spread quickly, with residents fighting to preserve their local environment. They were joined by members of the wider community who valued the area for its links with the early history of European settlement in Sydney. One of the earliest official statements opposing the development appeared in the City Council's Strategic Plan of 1971, which advocated rezoning The Rocks and developing it as a 'living museum'.[20] SCRA's brief was altered to take more account of the heritage qualities of the area, and over the next twenty years only a few of the planned high rise buildings materialised.

On the other hand, no one in Sydney had any power to prohibit demolition of buildings until the Wran Labor Government's Heritage Act was passed in 1977. This fact, in combination with a widespread community perception that 'heritage' was simply about saving buildings, and only the very old ones at that, meant that The Rocks redevelopment was unconcerned to conserve any of the post-1900 fabric, and today what remains there is only the oldest, infilled with modern 'sympathetic' buildings, decorated in so-called 'heritage colours'. It is an attractive tourist precinct, enveloping the visitor in an 'olde worlde' charm which bears little relationship to the actual past.

If the economic boom had lasted a little longer, Millers Point might well have become an extension of this tourist zone, and the same kind of thinking about what might be preserved and what removed would have prevailed. In 1971, the City Council, concerned at the absence of any controls over demolition, prepared a register of places which it believed ought to be preserved. In Millers Point, which it designated a 'residential precinct', the list was lengthy, but apart from the Walsh Bay wharves and the post office, it contained only nineteenth century buildings—the old pubs, Trinity Church, the Victorian terrace housing.[21] Similarly, a report to the Government on Observatory Hill in 1977 argued that the old houses in Kent Street should be restored, but said nothing about other structures.[22]

Indeed, Millers Point had lost some of its Harbour Trust houses, as well as some older stock, following the decision of the MSB to convert the finger wharves of Darling Harbour into longshore roll on/roll off container terminals. The first new wharf in this

---

20 NSCA CRS 75/3/1, *City of Sydney Strategic Plan*, 1971, p 88.
21 Ibid, p 144.
22 Final report to Hon N.K. Wran et al, 'The Development and Management of Observatory Hill', April 1977.

Walsh Bay, 1980s.

Reconstructing The Point. This photograph taken in 1972 shows how much has changed since 1937 (compare page 108). The big Dalgety's store has gone and the shoreline is being extended. Dibbs Street and Munn Street, both curving towards the new site, disappeared in the following years.

redevelopment project was built in 1964, and by the late sixties work was occurring at the end of The Point. The old Dalgety's wharf was reconstructed and the large 1903 stores which had stood on it were removed.[23] So was all the old housing on the west side of Merriman Street, including several of the former mansions that had characterised early Millers Point. Practically all of the housing in Munn Street disappeared, and the wide curve of the street itself was cut off, leaving only a short stretch of houses beside the Palisade Hotel. All that remains of the lost housing is a plaque commemorating its demise in the small grassed reserve.

Although there was local protest about these demolitions, there was suprisingly little over what Millers Point got in exchange—the Harbour Control Tower built in Merriman Street in 1974. In recognition of its role in berth control for the harbour, it is known as 'The Pill'. Its incongruity when viewed above the roofs of the houses in Dalgety Road or in conjunction with the Merriman Street cottages is so enormous that subsequent studies of the area tend to ignore it altogether, as if disbelieving that it is actually there.

When the building boom slowed to a halt in the second half of the seventies, it had touched Millers Point only lightly, but had not passed it by. High rise buildings had appeared in Kent Street, with the Esso building, which encroached furthest, replacing about half a dozen old sandstone cottages. More subtle, but indicative of the same pressure, was the trend towards leasing the old boarding houses in Lower Fort Street to professional and business organisations. But most of the area remained unchanged. The alterations to the wharves on The Point were not repeated for the Walsh Bay wharves, and eventually plans to upgrade them were shelved. An inquiry into the Maritime Industry in the mid-seventies made it clear that development was to concentrate on Port Botany, and by 1979 the National Trust had classified the Walsh Bay wharves and accompanying buildings.[24]

A resurgence of development activity in the city and its possible implications for Millers Point was signalled by the growth of tourism—real and hoped for—in the mid-eighties. To the east of Millers Point this resulted in accelerated activity in The Rocks, while to the south, enormous changes were heralded by the establishment of the Darling Harbour Authority in 1984. This body had been set up by the Labor Government in response to what it believed to be obstruction from the City Council over development of the large area of land vacated by the removal of the old Darling Harbour goods yards. Elements within the Council favoured developments which included housing and community facilities, while the Authority has presided over the creation of a major amusement and tourist complex of shops, restaurants and entertainment facilities.

But between these two developments stood Millers Point, by now peopled with residents skilled at making themselves heard. 'This highly organised and aware community is sensitive to intrusion' and understands that its neighbourhood needs to be 'protected and defended', wrote one of the ever-increasing number of consultants which, by 1985,

---

23 MSB, *Darling Harbour Redevelopment*, August 1974.
24 Commission of Enquiry into the Maritime Industry, 'Report on the Adequacy of Australia's Ports,' February 1976.

government departments were employing to advise them on the value of Millers Point.[25] A decade of quiet had allowed the newly formed Heritage Branch within the Planning and Environment Commission (now Department of Planning) to gather its strength and begin constructing a coherent picture of the significance of Millers Point. Planners at the City Council and state departments involved in administering the area began to formulate on paper the implications which flowed from the new claims which were being made that Millers Point was no ordinary place, nor even just a special place. Words like 'unique' began to be used. The significance of Millers Point, some were beginning to argue, lay not in its collection of early colonial buildings, nor in this or that site, but in its totality. This understanding was not shared by the Unsworth Labor Government, which announced in August 1985 that the MSB would lease the Walsh Bay wharves to private interests for redevelopment. The MSB immediately commissioned a planning study. This study recorded the importance of the wharves, which lay not only in their structure, but in their association with the work of the Sydney Harbour Trust, but while the preservation of the fabric of the wharves was not in dispute, the exercise was nevertheless premised on the assumption of redevelopment.[26]

In this same year, 1985, the MSB began the process of handing over its Millers Point housing to the Housing Commission (now Housing New South Wales). The transfer would take a number of years, and involved extensive renovation and repair of the buildings which, after years of MSB neglect, suffered 'stormwater entry, extreme weathering, footing subsidence, termite infestations, failing lath and plaster, poor draining, defective wiring and damaged fittings'.[27] Pronouncements of government authorities, redolent of the old post-plague days came back to haunt the residents of Millers Point. Their houses, they were told, were not good enough, and extensive upheavals would be necessary to fix them up.

As the new broom swept through this housing which had been administratively ignored for so long, there was inevitable disruption. In an attempt to be visible and accessible the Department of Housing set up an office in Windmill Street, and while some welcomed the new administration, it was inevitable that others would react angrily to the changes.

The most spectacular aspect of the transferral of control concerned the large residentials, for while some head tenants handed over administration of their houses to the Department in 1985, others resisted. Numerous court cases followed, with an attempt to have the properties resumed yet again being ruled invalid by the Supreme Court in 1987. Banners denouncing the Government appeared on the houses, and the press ran numerous articles about 'the war' which split the community of tenants. Combatants lined up for or against the ladies, who were characterised as kindly mother figures who provided an important role in sustaining their tenants, or as money-grabbing mercenaries who charged high rents for substandard accommodation. These events reflected the general unease felt by the

---

25 Wendy Sarkissian, for 'Social Planning Consortium 1985', Travis Partners Pty Ltd, Report to MSB for Walsh Bay EIS.
26 Travis Partners Pty Ltd, 'Walsh Bay Planning Study' for MSB, 1985.
27 John Gregory, 'Preliminary Strategy Plan Report, Millers Point', Dept. of Housing Urban Renewal Group, 1989.

From 1939 to the Present

From the MSB Tower may be seen almost all of the village of Millers Point. The CBD towers behind it.

community about replacing known ways of doing things by an impersonal bureaucracy. Tales of strong arm tactics, bumps in the night and illegal evictions abounded.[28]

But though this battle was dramatic and newsworthy, the more profound implications for the area affected by the Department of Housing's takeover arose from its policies of placing tenants. Initially the Department's criteria for placing tenants were relaxed to allow long-established residents to remain, but as places fell vacant they were filled from the normal Sydney-wide waiting list. Residents argued that this would destroy the community built on family ties and work relationships under the criteria used by the MSB. But there were problems with the old ways, too, indicated by empty wharves and under-utilised houses, and an increasingly ageing population. Official figures indicated that in 1986 19 per cent of the population was under twenty and 40 per cent was over fifty, compared with 30 per cent under twenty and 25 per cent over fifty in the whole of Sydney.[29] The total population was under a thousand people, with the predicted final population, after refurbishment, about 1,200. A return to the crowded conditions of 1947, when there were more than 1,500 people on the electoral roll—and that only accounted for those over twenty one—was now inconceivable and this considerable decrease in population indicates how much the area had changed.

---

28 For example, *Daily Telegraph*, 11 April 1985, 12 September 1987, 10 August 1989; *SMH*, 2 January 1987, 7 January 1987, 8 April 1989.
29 Australian Bureau of Statistics, 1986 Census, unpublished census district figures.

The wharves at Walsh Bay. Notice the contrast in scale of these early twentieth century buildings with the Moore's Wharf building, in the left foreground, built in the 1830s.

After it took control, the Department of Housing commissioned a number of studies of the area.[30] These said that just as the wharves were examples of significant engineering achievement, so too should the Harbour Trust's housing be preserved, and observed that the Trust's activities in the early decades of the twentieth century constituted 'an endeavour of national significance'. The whole of Millers Point should be retained 'as a cohesive example of nineteenth and early twentieth century townscape'.[31] The City Council's Draft Local Environment Plan for the city which appeared in 1986 did not go quite so far, but said similar things, defining the majority of the area as a 'Conservation Zone'.

Only a few years before, the significance of the Harbour Trust's work in the area had been largely ignored, and in the area administered by SCRA most of the early twentieth century buildings had been demolished. But eventually opinion was catching up with expressions of admiration which had been voiced early in the century and since forgotten. In 1914 a writer in *The Sydney Mail* had observed that in considering the activities of the Sydney Harbour Trust, 'one is struck not only by the magnitude of the work, but by the dignity of it. The Trust is doing its remodelling on aesthetic lines'.[32]

---

30 For example, Max Kelly, Kate Blackmore and Paul Ashton, 'Millers Point Housing Advice of Heritage Elements, Historical Survey', for Howard Tanner & Associates, July 1986; Terry Kass, 'A Socio-Economic History', May 1987.
31 'Millers Point Statement of Significance . . . ', Howard Tanner & Associates for NSW Dept. of Housing Inner City Project.
32 *Sydney Mail*, 28 January 1914.

From 1939 to the Present

All of these studies were moving towards the idea that what was at stake in Millers Point was its totality as a 'precinct', and increasingly there was an understanding that its degree of coherence was linked to the fact that ownership of the vast majority of places in Millers Point was in the hands of one landlord, the state. And, like many landlords, the state had taken little interest in improving or altering its houses. For decades the MSB had been more concerned to administer the functioning of the port than it had been to worry about the few hundred houses it had inherited from the time of the plague resumptions, and though this lack of interest had been often lamented by the residents, it meant that the housing stock had remained virtually unchanged since then.

But the notion of government ownership of property is not one which finds universal favour, and in March 1988 the Greiner Liberal Government came to power, with a strong commitment to privatisation and the disposal of government property which it considered could be better managed within the market economy. In the case of structures like school buildings or places like harbour foreshores this was bound to generate intense public debate, but in the case of random buildings acquired over the years through property resumptions and the like, it was assumed that such sell offs would not be problematic.

Except at Millers Point. In November 1988 the Department of Housing advertised the sale of two hotels, the old 1843 Hero of Waterloo, acquired by the Harbour Trust in the 1901 resumptions, and the Harbour View Hotel, built by the Trust in 1922. There were protests, which led to postponement of the sale until permanent conservation orders were placed on the buildings. This secured their retention as hotels, but did not stop them passing into private hands. The apparently reasonable policy of divesting the Department of Housing of its non-residential stock was at loggerheads with the growing lobby for the retention of Millers Point as a state-owned 'company town', a precinct. On 15 December

Above left: Harbour Trust housing, High Street, begun in 1910. *Above right*: The oldest houses in Millers Point, Glovers Cottages, built in the early 1820s.

Houses in Merriman Street. The end cottage was built in 1837. There is a detailed study of this house in Elizabeth Fink and Trevor Howells, 'Conservation of the West Rocks' (B. Arch. Thesis, Sydney University, 1974). In the foreground, where once stood the mansions of the Point, is Clyne Reserve.

1988 the Heritage Council formally requested that the Department of Housing make no further sales of government property before 'comprehensive consultation' with it.[33]

Despite this, at the beginning of April 1989, the Millers Point shops and the residential flats above them are advertised for freehold sale.[34] These little shops, subsidised by the Housing Department were the commercial centre of what was by now frequently referred to in the literature as 'the village of Millers Point'. Built by the Harbour Trust, they provided basic food and services and would almost certainly have been converted for more lucrative purposes if sold. For some it was a question of yet another 'assault on long term inner city residents in favour of developers'.

'All the tenants are in shock,' reported Sylvia McLeish, the president of the local tenants' association.[35] The state ALP member Sandra Nori and independent City Council alderman Frank Sartor were swift to condemn the proposed sale. When Sartor and a group of residents met with the head of the Housing Department, the *Herald* reported that this deputation was told that the Government had a philosophical commitment to selling commercial properties in the area.[36] The argument ran that by divesting itself of such

---

33 NSW Heritage Council, Minutes, 15 December 1988.
34 *SMH*, 1 April 1989 and subsequently.
35 *SMH*, 8 April 1989.
36 Ibid.

property the Department would gain additional funds for its proper role of providing public housing. But such an argument could be extended to almost all of Millers Point, or indeed to any form of public housing which did not conform to the criteria of cheapness and economy and could logically result in tracts of housing without commercial facilities. In the case of Millers Point, its supporters argued that this simplistic economic rationalism was inappropriate. The integrity of the whole precinct was under threat.

Support for retaining the shops was swift in coming. While building workers threatened green bans on any possible redevelopment, on 10 April 1989 the City Council unanimously opposed the sale, in what the press described as 'a rare show of cross factional unity'.[37] The Council also requested the Central Sydney Planning Committee to consider the zoning and heritage issues relating to Millers Point quickly, in advance of the general Sydney Local Environment Plan it was working on, and discussed the possibility of buying the shops in order to keep them in the public domain.[38] The following day Premier Greiner ordered the Department of Housing to reconsider, and three days later the Central Sydney Planning Committee unanimously rejected the sale of the shops. In the end, the buildings were leased to the Council to administer.

At the same time as all this was happening, there was a growing interest in the idea that Millers Point might be nominated for the World Heritage Register of UNESCO. This idea was being espoused by the local residents, by the local branch of the ALP, by the City Council and by the Federal Minister for the Environment, Senator Graham Richardson.[39] In June 1989, the historian of the Department of Planning's heritage Branch reported to the Heritage Council on this proposal. The precinct was, he said, 'definitely of national significance and most probably the outstanding urban place in Australia to qualify for such consideration'. The Heritage Council agreed to investigate the matter. It went further, in deciding to advise the Government that 'the subtleties of the heritage qualities are best maintained by Government ownership', at least until appropriate planning controls were worked out for such a complex issue as preserving an entire precinct.[40]

Securing Millers Point as a historic precinct was not going to be straightforward. At the beginning of the 1990s there were people living in Kent Street who looked out of their windows to a vast hole in the ground where a large tourist hotel was proposed to be built. The buildings which were demolished were not considered to be historically significant, but the structure which was proposed was not to be the anonymous, undatable infilling which is usually favoured in such circumstances. The hoarding around the hole was covered with the slogan 'Homes Not Hotels'.

Nor had the longstanding confusions over divided control been eradicated. The State Government was negotiating to return control of the streets to a reluctant City Council,

---

37 *Daily Mirror*, 12 April 1989; *SMH*, 11 April 1989.
38 RC, 10 April 1989.
39 Submission in support of a World Heritage Listing for Millers Point, Darling Harbour Branch of the ALP, May 1989; Senator Graham Richardson to David Hay, NSW Planning Minister, 20 April 1989.
40 A. Prescott, 'Report to Heritage Council Sub-Committee on Millers Point', 26 June 1989; NSW Heritage Council, Minutes, 3 August 1989.

ninety years after their resumption. The sticking point then, as in the 1930s, concerned the question of who will pay for current repairs.[41]

On the other hand, most of Millers Point was by now protected in some form or other. In mid-1989 the Central Sydney Heritage Inventory isolated it as 'a heritage precinct', and in 1990 the Department of Planning had commissioned a conservation study. These documents illustrated the enormous shift in thinking which had occurred in the last twenty years. The time for talking about the value of particular structures had passed, for

> *The most significant aspect of the place is its unity . . . It is not a building here or an archaeological deposit there—although individual items have been acknowledged as of very high significance. Rather, it is an immensely complex interaction between its architecture, archaeology, landscape, landform, location, past and present use, and, most importantly, its people. This very complexity demands something out of the ordinary when policies or developmental proposals affecting the area are being drawn up and it is of the utmost importance that the mistakes made in The Rocks are not repeated here.*[42]

In terms of cultural significance, the Department of Planning's statement of significance notes that 'the complex layering of activities and events, ranging from early colonial merchant and official enterprise to twentieth-century corporate port-town' is well documented both physically and 'by the experience and memory of its long-term community'. The 'technical and creative excellence of the period 1820–1930, including wharfage, warehousing, civic facilities and landscaping' is clearly in evidence, while the massive works of the Harbour Trust—which have remained largely unaltered since they were completed in the 1920s—leave 'virtually intact, residential areas, port and stevedoring works created . . . in response to the Sydney plague and the requirements of maritime trade at that time.'[43]

However, at the same time that this report was being written, the redevelopment of Walsh Bay was coming closer to reality, with the State Heritage Council approving the application of the developer CRI Ltd for an 'adaptive re-use scheme' which involved conversion of the wharves to residential apartments. The proposal also involved demolishing some of the bond stores and support buildings associated with the wharves, for which exemptions under the Heritage Act had to be made.[44]

The future of the Walsh Bay wharves was a complex issue, no matter how they were viewed along the spectrum of conservation to development. They were redundant to port operations by the early seventies, when it was widely assumed that they would have to be redeveloped, historical importance notwithstanding.[45] But when the MSB decided not to replace them with longshore berths, they entered a period of uncertain use or, more correctly,

---

41 NSCA CRS 326, S06-00247.
42 Kate Blackmore, et al, 'Millers Point Conservation Policy'. Department of Planning, February 1990; Thorpe Green & Associates/Anglin Associates for CCS, 'Heritage Inventory for Central Sydney', May 1989, Introductory Volume, p 48, sec 5.4.
43 A.Prescott, 'Statement of Cultural Significance for the Millers Point Precinct'. Department of Planning, 1990, sec 1.2, 1.3, 1.5.
44 Special meeting NSW Heritage Council, 17 August 1989.
45 NSCA CRS 75/3/1, *City of Sydney Strategic Plan*, 1971, p 88.

'... and most importantly, it's people'. The guest of honour is Sr Antoinette. Several of these people contributed reminiscences to this book.

disuse. Pier One was turned into a shopping and amusement complex in 1982 and in 1984 piers 4 and 5 were taken over by the Sydney Theatre Company for a theatre and restaurant. For the rest, short term tenancies were granted for storage and office space, with much of the huge storage area standing empty.[46] In these uses, the wharves had departed greatly from their intended use, and the meaning of 'conservation' took on a complexity beyond that which applied to the houses and buildings on the cliffs above. Gone were the great ships and the vast cargoes of wool. The pandemonium of comings and goings on Hickson Road had given way to long silences in the now wide spaces of the waterfront. It was in this context of uncertainty that the Unsworth Government announced that the wharves would be leased for private redevelopment, leading to the eventual acceptance of CRI's proposal in mid-1989.

The scheme made fewer overt changes to the structure of the buildings than other ideas for Walsh Bay which had been canvassed in recent years, but the development would have markedly altered the ambience of the precinct. The decision of the State Heritage Council to accept the proposal resulted in a protest meeting of locals at the Abraham Mott Hall in Argyle Place, and expressions of concern from the Australian Heritage Commission, now supporting the World Heritage idea.[47] The Conservation Policy study for Millers Point commissioned by the State Department of Planning stated that with this development pending for about thirty per cent of the area of Millers Point, the value of the whole

---

46 Planning Workshop, for CRI Ltd, 'Walsh Bay Redevelopment Statement of Environmental Effects', June 1989, Vol 1, pp 5–13.
47 *SMH*, 19 August 1989.

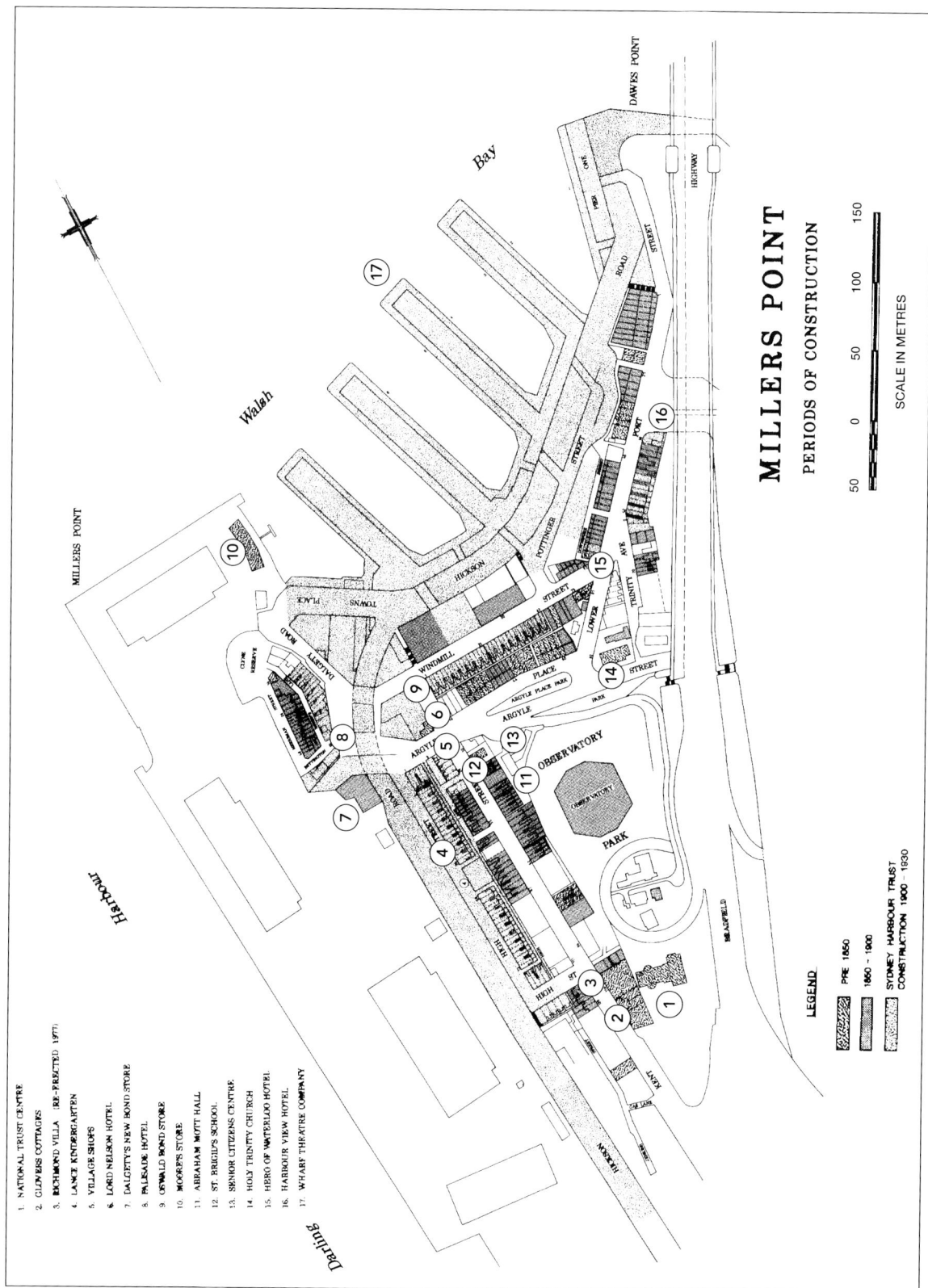

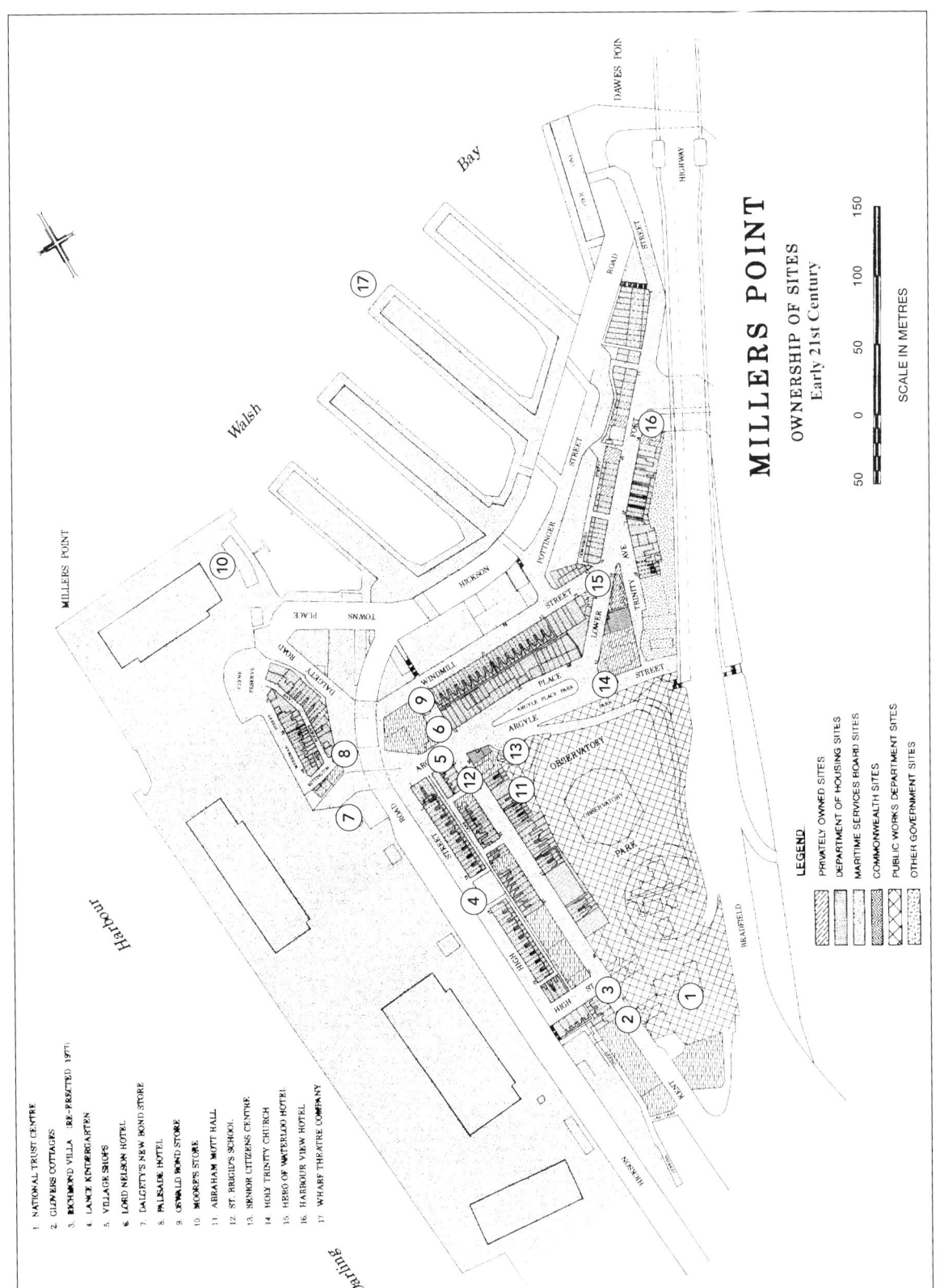

precinct was possibly diminished. The Planning Department's advice with regard to the World Heritage listing had been stronger:

> *The rarity and technological excellence of the Walsh Bay group is the factor which is most likely to qualify the precinct for World Heritage listing . . . If the scheme is approved in its present form there would be little value in further investigating the . . . proposal.*[48]

But while the developers were unconcerned about anything so esoteric as a World Heritage listing, other events, quite removed from any heritage considerations, were conspiring against the success of their proposal. Allegations of improper tendering practices on the part of the Government resulted in the project being considered by the Independent Commission Against Corruption in 1990. The findings of the Commission were inconclusive, but the timing of it and the general downturn in the economy were enough to induce the developers to withdraw. As has happened several times in preceding decades, economic expansion never quite reached Millers Point, and just as growth is being promoted as 'inevitable', contraction permitted a breathing space for considering the options. Questions of how best to use these wharves remained unresolved at the beginning of the 1990s. So Millers Point remained poised, its future uncertain.

Every minor incursion into the fabric of Millers Point generated extensive debate as the interests of tourism, residential amenity and heritage were juggled by various authorities and community groups. Often the substance of these concerns seemed trivial, but the struggle to 'get it right' for Millers Point was deemed worth the effort involved.

From the days when it was an outpost for sealers and smugglers, to its development as a vibrant sea port, through periods of social demise, and lately, with its star rising, there have always been people who have loved Millers Point, and looked upon it as a special place.

Look what's in my backyard! Steve Feeney c. 1960

---

48 A. Prescott, Report to Heritage Council Sub-Committee on Millers Point, 26 June 1989.

Postscript

At the conclusion of the first edition we observed that a slow down in the economic growth of Sydney had provided a breathing space where the significance of Millers Point could be reassessed in the light of a growing understanding of its importance as a heritage precinct, not because of 'this or that site, but in its totality' (p. 108, first edition, 1991). As earlier understandings of significance had been refined to include social and cultural values, and 20th as well as 19th century fabric, appreciation of Millers Point grew. The enormously important work of the Sydney Harbour Trust in the early twentieth century, and the virtual absence of development after 1930 had resulted in an intact and coherent place that was coming to be understood as unique.

In this context, the Greiner Liberal Government's decision to sell off the local shops in 1989 was reversed in the face of widespread concern, with the Heritage Council recommending retention in Government hands. MSB plans to replace the Walsh Bay wharves with modern facilities had been shelved as Port Botany became the main port of Sydney, and in 1988 a Permanent Conservation Order (PCO) had been placed on them and the surrounding area. Planning instruments were developed, and the Government sought bids for redevelopment, but with the caveat that all proposed works required the approval of its Heritage Council. A proposal by CRI Ltd was approved, but it fell foul of allegations of improper tendering, and by the time this had been formally investigated the economic viability was looking shaky. These plans were shelved in 1990.

That is where the story had got up to. The great Walsh Bay wharves and their shore sheds and stores stood practically empty, with their fabric slowly deteriorating as politicians, developers and concerned citizens debated their future use. Wharf 1 had been a shopping complex since 1981 and Wharves 4/5 were well established as performance and working spaces for the Sydney Theatre Company, but the remaining buildings were given over to short term tenancies or were vacant.

In 1994 the Government again sought proposals for reuse of the wharves, and in 1996 a panel of experts recommended acceptance of the tender of Walsh Bay Properties, a joint venture between Mirvac and Transfield. Having got the green light, this consortium promptly reported that deterioration of the wharves was worse than they had previously thought. They proposed demolishing Wharves 2/3 and 8/9. This was not acceptable under the heritage legislation which required that applications to demolish a 'whole building' subject to a PCO would be automatically refused.[1]

In 1997, Philippe Robert, a French urban designer with an international reputation in adaptation of existing buildings, was invited to consider the possibilities for Walsh Bay. His proposal emphasised heritage sensitivities, but the demolition of Wharves 6/7. Dilapidation claims were beginning to look a bit unconvincing, as the specifics of which wharves should

---

1 The MSB was disbanded in 1995 and its functions distributed to several new authorities. NSW Heritage Act, 1977, Sec 63 (2)(b).

be sacrificed shifted around the site. The termites were apparently fast moving. As well as rebuilding these wharves, the proposed new structure to replace Wharves 6/7 were to be severed from their connecting shore sheds, which would diminish the coherence of the complex, and result in something looking very much like a completely separate building.

Using Robert's advice, Walsh Bay Properties put in a new bid later that year, for apartments, commercial and retail space, and arts and cultural space including a major theatre. The Carr Labor Government's planning authority gave its consent, and a master plan was finally put on public display. Submissions from the public overwhelmingly opposed demolition of wharves 6/7.[2] Because the place was protected by a PCO a further consent was needed from the Heritage Council. This was given in early 1998, following the Heritage Council's acceptance of the argument of the Government Architect, Chris Johnson, that the whole of the Walsh Bay complex of wharves and shore sheds was one building, and that therefore demolition of one of the finger wharves did not constitute demolition of a building, but only part of a building.[3] The analogy of only severing one finger from the hand was used.

The Maritime Services Board control tower, referred to as 'The Pill' now administered by NSW Maritime.

Uproar followed. Heritage interests held rallies and meetings. The letters to the editor columns filled with impassioned views. Those who saw only a derelict precinct, with no alternative sympathetic use in the offing, and deterioration palpable, just wanted a solution that would revitalise the area, accommodate more people and provide jobs.

The proposed development involved substantial financial inputs from the Government, and the NSW Audit Office was highly critical of the processes, both planning and tendering, and of the lack of accountability. It was not reassured that the taxpayers would get value for money.[4]

The architectural fraternity was divided. Some saw a rare heritage gem, the only intact set of early twentieth century finger wharves remaining anywhere in the world. Others saw a structure worthy of being 'evolved'. A comparison to the many incarnations of the Louvre in Paris encouraged journalist David Marr to point out that 'the Louvre was built and rebuilt and restored in pursuit of State-funded, public, uncommercial, very French glory', whereas Walsh Bay was subject to 'the appetite for profit that's now at Sydney's throat.'[5]

---

2 New South Wales Audit Office, Performance Reports, 1998, Review of Walsh Bay, chronology of events, October 1997.
3 Heritage Council of NSW, 5 February 1998. It was argued that because the wharves were physically joined to the shore sheds by roof structures and decking they were not separate buildings.
4 New South Wales Audit Office, Performance Reports, 1998, Review of Walsh Bay.
5 David Marr, *SMH*, September 1998. Geraldine O'Brien, 'Harbour History Sellout Feared', *SMH*, 16 May 1998.

Postscript

The National Trust was outraged, and decided that the decision to demolish wharves 6/7 should be challenged in the courts. The case was set down for hearing in the Land and Environment Court on 13 May 1999. The Cabinet met early that morning, and an emissary was sent to the court to announce the Government's intention to introduce legislation to ensure validation of all consents already made for Walsh Bay. A bill was introduced into parliament that morning, and went straight into its second reading, with the Minister for Planning explaining that it was necessary to ensure the certainty of the Walsh Bay project, and to terminate the court action by the National Trust.[6] Morris Iemma, later to become Premier, argued that the legislation would end many years of 'frustration and delay in attempts to do something about Walsh Bay, a forgotten and neglected important heritage precinct of this city . . . the development is an important part of the Government's plan for this city post the Olympics. The bill is about job creation, heritage preservation and reopening this area of the city to the public for the first time since 1915.'[7] Any concerns over privatising this huge piece of public space were discarded as being obstructive and unrealistic, with the Government arguing the necessity for a partnership with private capital. In the end, practically everyone supported the bill in parliament. The Independent Clover Moore spoke angrily about the Government's actions that had taken state planning to 'a new low', undermining 'the independence and integrity of the courts [and] excluding public rights of appeal and participation in the development and future of this very important part of the public estate.'[8] But this was an argument about democracy. On the question of Walsh Bay itself most just wanted a solution. The proposed development promised to provide 2,000 jobs in a $650 million project that in six years would deliver a revitalised Walsh Bay that was not only vibrant and accessible, but, as was often claimed, '80% heritage'.

The redevelopment was enormously popular with those wealthy enough to buy into it. Many of the 239 new apartments in the new Wharves 6/7 and their shore buildings sold 'off the plan' in a matter of days in 2000, and when plans for thirty three 'Parbury Apartments' in Pottinger Street went on display in 2001, they were all snapped up in four hours. As increasing numbers of glass and light-filled new apartments permanently compromised the heritage significance of the area, promotion was always careful to emphasise its heritage strengths.

Old clay pipes, Chinese coins, and a harpoon head found when excavating Towns Place in 2002 decorate the lobby of the new building. The new Walsh Bay has won a number of design awards, including, perhaps ironically, a 2005 National Trust award for the Parbury Apartments and ruins. These archaeological remains, situated in the basement, the historical interpretations in the new Ferry Lane Park and the sensitive retention of much of the fabric of the working wharves ensure a positive and educative experience. The redevelopment of the wharves for expensive apartments and waterfront dining has

---

6 NSWLA, Hansard and Papers, 13 May 1999.
7 Ibid.
8 NSWLA, Hansard and Papers, 25 May 1999.

inevitably placed a gloss over the gritty working character of earlier times, but it has been done within a strong envelope of original wharf structures. Raw beams, relic machinery and interpretive storyboards go some way to tell the historical story.

What they do not make so explicit is the profound shift in the Sydney and the global economy that has made this transition a reality. A place once the site of hard labour, sweat and raw strength is now a place for strolling, enjoying a coffee, taking in a play at the Sydney Theatre Company's fine theatre on Hickson Road or joining in the literary discourse when the Sydney Writers Festival descends on the precinct once a year. Dancers practice their steps where hob nail boots once trod the boards.

This changing function has large implications for the older public housing of Millers Point. These houses and boarding houses have been in public hands for a century, home first to waterside workers' families, and since the late 1980s, to ordinary social housing tenants. While there are a number of heritage protections and listings for Millers Point, of individual buildings and of whole conservation areas, none of this will ensure maintenance of the kind of community that has historically lived in Millers Point.

Retaining public tenants would help, but for a housing authority with a brief to provide for the needy, the cost of maintaining expensive building fabric in this historic enclave is not an obvious first priority. Early reassurances that these houses would remain as public housing have been watered down over time, and the practice of recent years has been to lease properties on ninety nine year leases, albeit with strict requirements to conserve them, to private interests. The first to go this route were commercial buildings, including the shops that Greiner was unsuccessful in selling in the 1980s. When the release of sixteen houses on long term lease was announced in late 2007, Housing NSW did not mention their working class origins, but positioned them as 'prestigious, heritage-listed properties… located in a stunning part of the city'.[9] While this approach may be good for restoring the building stock, it will of course, over time, alter the social mix of residents so that any connections to an older, working population may become lost. Future tenants may have more in common with the newer residents of Walsh Bay than they will have with past residents of Millers Point. Retaining this most significant and intact worker enclave is now a lost possibility. Moving to the next phase of creating a place of social mix is a challenge that faces all inner city locations, but to lose it here in Millers Point would be more of a severance with the past than anywhere else in Sydney.

Currently, there is another point of pressure developing on the older residential area of Millers Point, coming from plans to create a new urban precinct on the Millers Point end of Darling Harbour.

Back in 1998, while the fate of Walsh Bay was being debated, on the other side of Millers Point a struggle of a different order was unfolding. The Federal Howard Government had taken secret steps to train defence personnel overseas in Dubai in order to undermine the Maritime Union of Australia (MUA). The stevedoring company Patricks, headed by Chris Corrigan, attempted to sack the whole of its unionised workforce on the evening of 7 April

---

9 Housing NSW, press release, 12 November 2007.

in preparation for bringing in non-union labour. The following day waterside workers around Australia struck and pickets were established at ports, including at the Patricks gates on Hickson Road in Millers Point. This piece of waterfront had witnessed many savage maritime and wharf strikes in its turbulent history, but the vehemence and brutality of this particular confrontation was a new experience for many Australians, who watched the whole saga on their televisions. Fellow travellers and supporters went down to Hickson Road to stand in solidarity, contribute to the communal bucket collection, hear the Trade Union Choir sing and join in the defiant chant of 'MUA, here to stay'.

Two months later, after international support, an agreement was reached between the union and Patricks, with legal charges against Patricks dropped in exchange for Patricks agreeing to abandon attempts to replace the Union workforce and to retain award conditions.

Since 1998, these events have been remembered in documentary film, writings and song. When the Sydney Theatre Company opened at its brand new theatre in Hickson Road during the 2004 Sydney Festival, the performance was Katherine Thompson's fictitious *Harbour*, based on the real life drama of the strike which had been played out in reality a few hundred metres up the road. On 8 April 2008, a decade on from the strike, one minute's silence was observed on the wharves around Australia, and also at the Sydney Convention Centre in Darling Harbour, where 500 delegates were attending an MUA national conference. The same week a Laborfest at Darling Harbour celebrated the success of the workers, with poetry and images, and singers performing 'Pickup Shed', 'Join the MUA' and 'Bring out the Banners'.[10]

But down at Patricks, the silence had already fallen, and the gates were locked against vandalism. Since 1998 the ongoing contraction of the waterside workforce was compounded by the virtual closure of Port Jackson as a working port. The Hungry Mile, so long the lifeline of the community of Millers Point, was an empty expanse of wide road, waiting . . . for what?

The first taste of what is to come was evident in the modern Bond development on Hickson Road, a mixture of prestige commercial and residential buildings. Then in 2005–06 the Government held an international design competition to come up with proposals for a 22 hectare site of surplus wharfage in East Darling Harbour. A team of Sydney-based architects won the contest with a concept that gave over half the site to a headland park, ensured continuous public access to the water and emphasised reconnecting this part of the city back into the whole. Options for maintaining small and not so small maritime activities were canvassed. Talk of a ferry terminal revived maritime uses that had been foreclosed on at Walsh Bay.

But concept proposals have given way to arguments in favour of increased density, and increased commercial components, fuelling fears of a place that is 'fearsome at night' and 'a wasteland on weekends'.[11] As this postscript is being written, the Government's Sydney

---

10 Details at www.mua.org.au under Laborfest.
11 Jahn Gehl, *ABC News*, Thursday 17 April 2008. Gehl is a Danish planner who was brought to Sydney to advise the City of Sydney on urban design and sustainability issues in 2007.

Harbour Foreshore Authority, which will manage development on this huge new site, has submitted modifications to the plans which increase the densities, increase the commercial components, and probably also threaten the views from older housing in the elevated parts of Millers Point. The winners of the design proposal have been vehement in their objections to the way things have progressed since the design was first released, arguing that sensitive public and civic design has been jettisoned in favour of a 'monoculture of bulky office buildings.'[12]

The population of Millers Point at the time of first writing this book was around 1,000 people. The Department of Housing wanted to get this up to around 1,200. By 2001 it stood at almost 1,600 and by 2006 it was just over 3,000. This will increase enormously with the new development.

But it won't be counted as part of Millers Point. The name has been under constant attack since the bus destinations and the Post Office were renamed The Rocks back in the 1980s. When this ploy met with a storm of local protest the name Millers Point reappeared. But then in 1993 part of it was officially gazetted as Dawes Point. And Walsh Bay emerged as a residential name, though with some of it officially in Millers Point, and some in Dawes Point. And this newest precinct facing East Darling Harbour has been officially named Barangaroo. When Pope Pius Benedict XVI came to Sydney for World Youth Day in July 2008 he inadvertently promoted this government-generated name because many of the events, including the finale of the re-enactment of the crucifixion of Christ were located at Barangaroo. As the name fell from his lips this was the first time many Sydneysiders had consciously registered it. The wharf labouring fraternity and a lot of people with a sense of history want it to be called the Hungry Mile. So does *The Sydney Morning Herald*, which uses this name in newspaper reportage.

Another possible name is Millers Point. However this would extend the area that currently has this name a little, and the official aim seems to be to obliterate or at least emaciate it. The current practice of referring to 'Dawes Point' and 'Walsh Bay' and now 'Darling Harbour East/ Hungry Mile/Barangaroo' as separate places contributes to confused thinking that misses the tightly integrated history of the area. This is part of repositioning the area for a prosperous 21st century future, and forgetting its connections to a harsher and poorer past. If a little book like this assists to keep alive memories of a Millers Point that is rapidly becoming lost, then it will have served some small purpose.

---

12 The winning team was Hill Thallis, Architecture + Urban Projects, Paul Berkemeier Architects and Jane Irwin, Landscape Architecture. Sunanda Creagh, 'Hungrier Mile ruins prize site: architects', *Sydney Morning Herald*, 5 August 2008; Barangaroo Update at www.hillthalis.com.au.

Sources of Illustrations

Page

6	Steps to Dalgety Street (CCS, photographer Paul Patterson)
7	St Brigid's School fete
8	Watson Road (CCS, Photographer Paul Patterson)
11	*Vue de Millers Point, Sydney*, 1845, Eugene Delessert (ML SLNSW and Dixon Gallery)
12	Ship, Sydney Cove, 1803 (National Library of Australia)
13	Bradley's map, 1788 (ML SLNSW)
14	*Fort on point of Sydney Harbour*, Rebecca S. Hall, 1840 (ML SLNSW SPF)
16	*Millers Point*, Samuel Elyard, nd (ML SLNSW SPF)
18	Harper's map of Sydney, c. 1825 (SRNSW)
19	*Northern View of Sydney in the Twenties*, H.W. based on Lycett? (ML SLNSW SPF)
22	Sketch of Millers Point in 1831, Surveyor General's Sketch Books (SRNSW)
24	Eber Bunker (ML SLNSW SPF)
25	Wood & Sons advertisement, in W.J. Dakin, *Whalemen Adventurers in Southern Waters* (Angus & Robertson, Sydney, 1977)
26A	Henry Moore, nd (ML SLNSW SPF)
26B	Robert Towns, nd (ML SLNSW SPF)
28A	Clyde Bank, in Cumberland County Council, *Historic Buildings Central Area of Sydney*, Vol 2 (Cumberland County Council, Sydney, 1962)
28B	*Argyle Street*, J.B. Henderson, nd (ML SLNSW SPF)
30	Albion House, Millers Point, c. 1840s (ML SLNSW SPF)
35	Clyde Street, 'Views Taken During Cleansing Operations, Quarantine Areas 1900 . . .' (ML SLNSW MS)
38	St Phillips Church, Joseph Fowles, *Sydney in 1848* (facsimile edition, Ure Smith, Sydney, 1962)
39	Fort Street School, Joseph Fowles, *Sydney in 1848* (facsimile edition, Ure Smith, Sydney, 1962)
40	Dawes Battery, 1842 (ML SLNSW SPF)
41	Lord Nelson Hotel, Argyle Street, nd (ML SLNSW SPF)
44	Ships at anchor, Sydney Cove, nd (ML SLNSW SPF)
45	Cuthbert's shipyard, 1873 (Holtermann Collection, ML SLNSW SPF)
47A	*Vue de Millers Point, Sydney*, 1845, Eugene Delessert (ML SLNSW and Dixson Gallery)
47B	*Sydney in the Forties*, Joseph Fowles (ML SLNSW)
50	Walsh Bay waterfront, nd (ML SLNSW SPF)
53	Kent Street, nd (ML SLNSW SPF)
54	*Gas Works from Millers Point*, Samuel Elyard, nd (ML SLNSW SPF)
56	Cuthbert's shipyard, 1871 (ML SLNSW SPF)
57A	Dibbs's Wharf, nd (ML SLNSW SPF)
57B	T.A. Dibbs, nd (ML SLNSW SPF)
59	Wool carts, Free labourers at work on wharves during strike, 1917 (ML SLNSW GPO1)
61	*Millers Point*, c. 1870s, Samuel Elyard (ML SLNSW SPF)
63	Millers Point map, 1880 (CCS)
66	Parbury's Wharf, 1895 (ML SLNSW SPF)
68	Larry Foley, nd (ML SLNSW SPF)
69	The Millers Point Push on trial (*Bulletin*)

70	Fire at Hentsch's bond store, 1903 (Joyce Phillips private collection)
71	Millers Point at the turn of the century (Stanton Library)
72	*Clyde Street*, 1902, Sydney Long (ML SLNSW)
74	Clyde Street, 'Views Taken During Cleansing Operations, Quarantine Areas 1900' (ML SLNSW MS)
77	*Millars Point* (sic), Lionel Lindsay (ML SLNSW SPF)
78	Plague cleanup, Walsh Bay, 1900 (ML SLNSW GPO1)
80	R.R.P. Hickson (ML SLNSW)
83	Windmill Street, c. 1904 (ML SLNSW SPF)
84	Clyde Street, 'Views Taken During Cleansing Operations, Quarantine Areas 1900' (ML SLNSW MS)
85	Varney Parkes (ML SLNSW)
86	Retaining wall, Millers Point (ML SLNSW GPO1)
87	Bridge spanning Hickson Road (ML SLNSW GPO1)
90	Photographer: Paul Patterson (CCS)
91A	New Pottinger Street, 1922 (ML SLNSW GPO1)
91B	No. 1 Wharf (ML SLNSW GPO1)
93	Men working, corner of Towns Place (Joyce Phillips private collection)
94	No. 8–9 Walsh Bay, 1917 (ML SLNSW GPO1)
96	Unloading potatoes (WWF)
97	*Waterfront Workers*, Harold Greenhill, 1946 (GPO1)
99	Fort Street School, 1919 (Joyce Phillips private collection)
100	Labourers on wharf, 1917 (ML SLNSW GPO1)
103	Coal lumpers (WWF)
105A	St Michaels (St Brigids, Heritage Gallery, Kent Street)
105B	Fr Piquet (St Brigids, Heritage Gallery, Kent Street)
107	Painters, Sydney Harbour Bridge, 1931 (ML SLNSW)
108	Darling Harbour, 1937 (ML SLNSW and Tourist Commission of NSW)
109	Jim Healy (WWF)
111	Margins campaign, 1956 (WWF)
112	Cargo in Hickson Road (ML SLNSW GPO1)
115	Kitchen scene (Joyce Feeney (née Doohan) private collection)
117	Tony Bradford (CCS, CRS80/160)
118	Second class, Fort Street School (Joyce Feeney private collection)
120A	Walsh Bay, 1980s (Paul Patterson private collection)
120B	Darling Harbour, 1972 (ML SLNSW and Tourist Commission of NSW)
123	Millers Point from the MSB Tower (CCS, photographer Adrian Hall)
124	Walsh Bay Wharves (CCS, photographer Adrian Hall)
125A	High Street (CCS, photographer Adrian Hall)
125B	Glovers Cottage (CCS, photographer Adrian Hall)
126	Merriman Street (CCS, photographer Adrian Hall)
129	Women at birthday party (St Brigids, Heritage Gallery, Kent Street)
130	Millers Point—Periods of Construction (CCS)
131	Millers Point—Ownership of Sites (CCS)
132	Child, Observatory Park (Joyce Feeney private collection)
134	Harbour control tower (CCS, photographer Paul Patterson)

INDEX

A
Aborigines 7, 9, 10
Abraham Mott Hall 100, 117, 129
Agar, Thomas 23
Agar St. 98
Albion House **30**, 31, 40
Alfred Terrace 54
Allen, Stephen
Antoinette, Sr **129**
Argyle Cut 7, **28**, 33, 42, 68, 98, 108
Argyle Place 19, 23, 54, 60, 62, 100, 104, 117, 129
Argyle St. **8**, 17, 19, 28, 30, 32–33, 39–40, **41**, 43, 62, 68, 86, **87**, 88–9, 106
Askin Government 118
Aspinall Brown & Co. 24, 32, 33, 49
Austin, E.W. 88
Australian Gas Light Co. 34, 36, **54**, 55, 90–92
Australian Labor Party 67, 88, 109, 116–117, **117**, 126, 127

B
Ball, Harry **103**
Barangaroo 138
Barnett, Charles 55
Beckett, 'Big Joe' 103
Berry Alexander 21, 24, 25
Bettington, J.B. 23, 24, 55
Bettington St. 16, 36, 55, 59
Bettington's Wharf 30, 31
Big House Hotel 90
Bigge, J.T 20, 23, 49
Bingle, John 24
Black Dog Hotel 38
Blacket, Edmund 55
blacksmiths 56, 114
Blacksmiths Arms 41
Bland, William 43
boarding houses 7, 29, 31, 38, 46, 50, 54, 81, 89, 97, 114, 116, 121, 136
Boatwright, Mrs. 40
Bond, John Pomroy 41
bond stores (see warehouses)
Botts, W.C. 49–50, 55–6
Bott's Wharf 24
Bourke, Sir Richard (Governor) 39
Boyce Charles 73
Bradfield, Dr. J.J.C. 80
Bradford, Tony **117**
Brady, E.J. 62–4, 66–7
Britain, British 10, 14, 23, 25, 43, 48, 95, 97
Brodsky, Isadore 68
Brooks & Co. 27
Brooks, Robert 48
Brown, Mrs. (ladies school) 40
Bryant, Lucy 17
Bryce, Matthew 23
Buchanan, Walter 24
Bunker, Eber **24**, 25
Bunker's Hill 25, 40
Busby's Bore 33, 51
'Busy Bee' (restaurant) 114
butchers 17, 55
Byrnes, Ellie 89

C
Callaghan, Patrick 107
Calwell, Arthur 109
Campbell, James 59
Campbell, Robert 19
Campbell, Robert, Jnr. 29
Carlson Terrace 60
carpenters 29, 48, 51, 54
Carr Government 134
Centenary Café 114
Central Wharf 56 7, 69, 101
Chambers, C.H. 34
Chapman, W.H. 23, 33
children 15, 17, 40–1, 61, 74, 74, 89, **99**, 104–6, 111, 113, 115, 116, **118**, **132**
China, Chinese 24, 26, 49, 98, 135
Chippendale 35
Church Hill 39, 40
churches **28**, 38–40, 42, 55, 61, 81, 97, 109, 112, 117, 119
Chusan 48
Circular Quay 33, 75, 113
Clancy, Michael 55
Clarke, John 20, 21
Clyde Bank **28**, 29
Clyde St. **29**, 30, 34, **35**, 36, 41, 56, 59, **72**, **74**, **84**
Clyne, D. 117
Clyne Reserve 31, **126**
Coal Lumpers Hall 100 (see also Abraham Mott Hall)
Cockatoo Island 46
Cockle Bay Point 9, 16
Communist Party 67, 102, 109
Connaghan, Molly 81, 104, 111
conservation 119, 122, 124–5, 127–9, 135–6
convicts 7, 9, 10, 23, 32, 33, 39, 43, 46
Coodye 9, 11
Corcoran, Lawrence 32
Corcoran's Shipyard 36, 50

Corrigan, Chris 136
Crawford, Robert 29
CRI Ltd. 128, 129, 133
Cribb, Tom 17
crime 37, 43–4, 68, **69**, 106, 132
Crook, John 52
Crown Rd. 36–7, **41**, 53–4 (see also Merriman St.)
Cumberland St. 33, 43, 61, 90
Cuthbert, John 32, 50, 51, 55, 56
Cuthbert's Shipyard **45**, **57**, 58

D
Dalgety & Co. 49, 64, 66, 69, 94
Dalgety Rd. 27, 34, 93, 121 (see also Moore's Rd.)
Dalgety Terrace 16, 31, 34, 88, 114
Dalgety's bond stores 64, 69, **108**, **120**
Dalgety's Wharf 49, 56–7, 62, 66, 69, 90, 121
Dalton's Wharf 57, 69
Dansey, George 60
Darley, Benjamin 31
Darling Harbour 9, 11, 17, 19, 20, 23, 24, 25, 31, 34, 42, 43, **45**, 48, **54**, 55, 59, 65, 75, 77, 80, 83, 88, 90–91, 95, 100, 116, 119, 136–7
Davies, William 31
Davies Terrace 55
Davis, Mr. (landowner, 1840s) 16
Davis, William 39
Dawes Battery **14**, 15, 40, **40**, 43, 77
Dawes Point 9, 10, 11, 16, 17, 18, **19**, 21, 39, **66**, 77, 88, 90, 91, **91**, 138
Dawes, Lt. William 15
Deloitte, Capt. 55
demolition **74**, 82–3, **83**, 84–90, **91**, 105, 119, 121, 124, 127–8, 133–5
depressions 24, 35, 37, 48, 62, 66–7, 90, 95, 101, 102, 104, 106, 109, 112–3
Dibbs, T.A. **56**, 56, 67
Dibbs St. 31, 120
Dibbs's Wharves 56, **57**, 57–8, 69, 90
disease 10, 60, 71, 73, 74
Downton & Dyer 106
Dudley, James Riley 75
Duguid & Co. 55
Duke's Wharf 24
Dumbarton Castle Hotel 90

E
East India Company 23–5
Ebsworth & Co. 49

Ebsworth's Wharf 55
Edwards, Mr. 31
Ellis, Mrs. 104
employment and unemployment 20, 25, 27, 35–7, 42, 54, 58, 64, 66–7, 88, 94 6, 100–2, 106, 109
Erskine St. 17
Essex St. 81
Esso Building 121

F
Fairfax, Sir James 42
Faris, Joseph 32, 41, 52
Farrell, Mary 36
Farrer, Mrs. 105
Ferry Lane 73
Ferry Lane Park 135
Flagstaff Hill 15, 17, 43 (see also Observatory Hill)
Flood & Co. 49, 64
Flood, Edward 39
Flood's Wharf 55, 58
Foley, Larry **68**
Fort Phillip 9, 15, 17, **19**, 28
Fort St. 17, 34, 86
Fort Street Model (High) School 15, **39**, 40, 61–2, **99**, 105
Fort Street Primary School 117, **118**

G
Gaby, James 101, 110
Gallagher, Bill 114
Garran, Andrew 57–8
'Garrison Church' (Holy Trinity) 28, 39–40, 42, 55, 61, 81, 97, 109, 112
Geoghegan, Edward 42
George St. 88, 106, 114
Gilchrist Watt & Co. 56
Ginn, Henry 39
Gladstone Hotel 68–9
Gloucester St. 34, 41
Glover, Thomas 29, 36, 59, **125**
Go-mo-ra 9
Goss, 'Granny' 104
Govett, William 42
Grafton Bond Store 69
green bans 118, 127
Greiner, Nick 125, 136
Griffiths, John 55
Grosvenor St. 16, 39
Gwynne-Hughes, Dr. 76

H
Hallen, Ambrose 20
Harbour Control Tower 31, 121, **123**, **136**
Harbour View Hotel 61, 90, **90**, 125
Harris, Alexander 16, 20
Harris, John 61–2

Harris's bakery 55
Harry Jensen Centre 117
Hart St. 60, 73, 89
Hashemy 25
Hawkely, Edward 39
health and hygiene 59–60, 69–71, 103–4
Healy, 'Big Jim' **109**
Henry, Cecil 107
Hentsch, W.H. 69
Hentsch's Bond Store **70**
Heritage Council 126–7, 133–4
Hero of Waterloo Hotel 21, 41–2, 44, 61, **91**, 125
Hescot, George 17
Hesham Terrace 54
Hickson, R.R.P **80**, 81, 85–6, **86**
Hickson Rd. 73, **74**, 87, **87**, 90–2, **112**, 129, 134, 137
Higgins, Justice H.B. 98
High St.73, 81, **87**, 89, 105, **125**
Hit or Miss Hotel 61, 90, **91**
Holden family 60
Holy Trinity ('Garrison Church') 28, 39–40, 42, 55, 61, 81, 92, 104, 112
Hosking, John 23
hotels 34, 38, 41–2, 46, 90, 125
housing 8, 12, 19, **28**, 28–9, **35**, 36, **50**, **53**, 54–5, 59–60, **61**, 78–9, 81 90, 92, 97, 108, 112–4, 117, 119, 121–2, 124–5, **125**, 127, 136
Housing Board (Housing Commission, Department of Housing, Housing N.S.W.) 8, 89, 133, 122–6
Howard Government 136
Hughes, J.T. 23, 29
Hughes, W.M. 76, 98–9
Hunter, John (Governor) 10, 16
Hungry Mile, The 96, 137–8

I
Iemma, Morris 135
Irish 15, 30, 89
Irving, John 23
Isaacs, J.L. 58

J
Jack the Miller 9, 16–7, 19, 21, 23
Jackson, May 117
Jenkins, Elizabeth 23
Jenkins St. **54**, 55
Jensen, Harry 116
Jobson, James 55
Johnson, Chris 134
Johnson, Mr. (boarding house) 31
Jones, John 16, 43
Jones, Ray **111**
Jones, Richard 25

Jones & Walker 27
Jones's Wharf 24, 26, 37
Jubughalee 10

K
Kent St. 9, 17, 18, 21, 23, 28, 31, 34, 36, 39, 41, 42, 52–5, **53**, **54**, 59–60, 62, 73, 81, 86, **87**, 88–9, 91, 99, 104–5, 114, 119, 121, 127
Kent Street Model Lodging House 61, 99
King, Philip Gidley (Governor) 15
King St. 73
King's Wharf 19
Klapdor, Helen 112–3

L
labour movement 64, 67, 98–103, 110–1
labour 29 32, 36–7, 42, 50–1, 54, 56, 58, 62, 64, **93**, 94, **96**, **97**, 96–97, **100**, 102–104, 116
Lag's Jetty 46
Lamb, Alfred 56, 69
Lamb, John 21, 24, 28, 31, 36, 55
Lamb (Alfred) & Co. 64
Lamb Parbury & Co. 24, 49–50, 56
Lance Kindergarten 89
Lane, Timothy 33
Lang, Rev. J.D. 30
larrikin pushes 43, **68**, 68–9, **69**
Leighton, David 20, 30
Leighton, John 9, 16, 17, 19, 21, 23
Lewis, Mortimer 40
Little Sisters of the Poor 105
Live and Let Live Hotel 61
Loftus St. 60
Long, Sydney **72**
Long, William 21, **26**, 27
Long's Wharf 26, 31
Long and Wright's Wharf 98–9
Lord Nelson Hotel **30**, 41, **41**, 42
Lowe, Joseph 17
Lower Fort St. 19, 29, 31, 36, 37, 39 42, **47**, **50–1**, 52, 54, 57–8, 60–2, 73, 81, 89, 97, 104, 114, 121
Lucas, Nathaniel 16
Lucas & Wall 16
Lumber Wharf 24
Lyne, W.J. 76
Lynx 25

M
McBride, Mr. 98–9
McDonald, Vera 104, 113
Macdonald, William David, Jnr and Snr 114
MacIntosh Hughie 103
McKeon, Humphrey 43

McKillop, Ramsay 64
Maclehose, J. 28–30
McLeish, Sylvia 126
McMillan, John 32
Macnamara, John 49–50, 55–6
Macnamara's Wharf 48, 56
Macquarie, Lachlan (Governor) 19, 21
McQueen, Dr. Roland 103
McRoberts, Mr. 40
maps and plans **14, 18, 22, 63, 79, 130, 131**
Maritime Services Board (MSB) 8, 31, 105, 108, 111, 113–4, 116, 119, 122–5, 128
Market Wharf 20, 25
Marmount, Patrick 21
Marsden, George 55
Marsden, Rev. Samuel 49
Martin, Arthur 23
Martin, J.B. 42, 46
Martin, Nurse 104
Mary (ship) 25
Maxwell, Ron **111**
Melville, Capt. Thomas 25
merchants 7, 19, 20, 23–4, 25–8, 37, 48–50, 54, 55, 58
Merriman, Mrs. 98
Merriman St. 16, 31, 33, 36, **41**, 55, 59, 114, 116, 121, **126** (see also Crown Rd)
Merriman Terrace **41**, 53
Millers Rd. (Millers Point Rd.) 30, 34, 41, 55, 73
Milton Terrace 54
Minogue, Dan 116
Moon, Henry 58
Moore, Henry 23, **26**, 27, 29, 31, 35, **44**, 49–50, 53, 55, 58, 62
Moore, Joseph 23, 27 9
Moorecliff 31, 38
Moore's Bond Store 27
Moore's Cooperage 32
Moore, Clover 135
Moore's Rd. 27, 36, 41, 55, 58, 62, 68
Moore's Wharf 48–9, 56–58, 69, **124**
Moran, Stan **111**
Mott's Hall 106
Mullins, Barney 101
Mundy, G.C. 42–3
Munn, James 23, shipyard 30
Munn St. 23, 30, 36, 52, 55, 69, **87**, 89, **120**, 121
Murphy, James 55

N
Napoleon Inn 42, 55
National Trust 121, 134
Nelson, Tom 68, 100
New South Wales Government 75, 77, 80–4, 88–9, 98–9, 113, 127
Nori, Sandra 126

O
O'Brien, Mary 39
O'Brien, Mrs. 114
Observatory, The 9, 15, 30, 58, **71**
Observatory Hill 11, 15, 16, 82, 86, 114, 119
Observatory Park **8**
O'Connell, Captain Daniel 43
O'Connell, Mr. 51
Old Whalers Arms 41
Olsen, Elsie (née Solomon) 104
Oswald's Bond Store 69

P
Pacific Islands 26–8, 46, 49
Palisades Hotel 90, 121
Parbury's Wharf **66**
Parkes, Varney 85, **85**
Paton, George 36, 41–2
Patrick Stevedores 136–7
Payne, Arthur 73
Perrier, Mrs. 40
Pert, Tom 68–9, **69**
Phillip, Capt. Arthur 10, 12
Phillips, Joyce 81
Piquet, Father **105**
Pittman, T.G. 21
Pittman's Wharf 24
plague (see also disease) 71, 73–80, 128
Planning Department 122, 127–130
Point Maskelyne 15
policing 21, 43, 65, 99, 101, 104, 106
Port Botany 121, 133
Port Jackson 10, 23, 137
Pottinger St. 52, 55, 58, 91, **91**, 135
Princes St. 33, 40, 52, 80–1, 90
prostitution 7, 20, 29, 38, 116
protests 119, 121–2, 134
Public Works Department 80, 84–5, 87, 89
pubs 34, 38, 41–2, 46, 90, 125

Q
quarantine 60, 75–6
Quarantine Station 60, 73
Quarries, The 17, 19, 28
Quarryman's Arms 41

R
Rae, John 16
Rainbow Inn 41
redevelopment 90, 117–121, 135, 137–8
Redgrave, John 32

Reid, George 81
Richard Brooks & Co. 27
Richardson, Senator Graham 127
Robert, Philippe, 133–4
Roberts, C.J. 60
Rocheford, Mr. 17
Rocks, The 7, 9, 11, 20, 25, 32, 35, 38–9, 41, 43, 60, 77, 81, 89–90, 93, 98, 108, 114, 118–9, 121, 138
Roden's Lane 114
Royal Oak Hotel 41, **41**
Royal Victoria Theatre 42, 43

S
St. Brigid's Church and School (St. Bridget's) 7, 39, 61, 105
St Joseph, Sisters of 61
St. Michael's Church and Orphanage 61, **105**
St Patrick's Church and School 39, 105
St Philip's Church (St Phillip's [sic]) **38**, 39
Sainty, Mrs. 98
Sartor, Frank 126
school **7**, 15, 38–40, **39**, 60–1, **99**, 115–7, **118**
Scotch Row (see also Clyde St.) **29**, 30
sealing 14, 25, 132
seamen 7, 27–8, 31 2, 37–8, 41–6, 50, 53, 61, 65, 96–8, 101–2, 114, 116
Selfe, Norman 56, 81
sewerage and drainage 33, 35, 52, 59, 69
Sheer Hulk Hotel 38
Shepherd and Alger's Wharf 24
shipbuilding 19, 32, 36, 50 1
shipping 10, 14, 21, 24–6, 29, 31–3, 35, 37, 48–9, 56, **59**, 65, 77–8, 90, 93–6, **94**, 98, 102, 109, 112
Shipwright's Arms 41
Sloss, A. 117
Smith, Charles 55
Smith, Lillian 106
Smith, Thomas 52
Smith's Paddock 59
Smith's Road 62
Smith's Wharf 57–8
social life 42–3, 48, 65, 105, 108, **115**
Spark, A.B. 23
Spencer Lodge 31, 36, 58
Spruson, W.J. 76
Steam Packet Hotel 41
stevedores 32, 56, 64–5, 101–2, 110
Stevens, J.M. 61
Stewart (J.) & Co. 81
stonemasons 30, 32, 42–3

strikes 65, 67–8, 95, 98–9, **100**, 102, 137
Stuart, Alexander 31
Stubbs, John 33
Stubbs (auctioneer) 42
Summerbell, Andrew 32
Summerbell's Wharf 60
Sussex St. 17, 32, 35, 75, 92, 96, 104
Sydney City Council 33–4, 36, 51–2, 58, 60, 62, 67, 69–71, 73–5, 77, 80–3, 87–9, 92–3, 97, 113, 119, 121–2, 124, 126, 127
Sydney Cove 9–10, 12, 14–6, 19–21
Sydney Harbour Bridge 7, 15, 61, 80, 90, **90**, **107**, 108, 118, **118**
Sydney Theatre Company 129, 133, 136–7

T
Talbot & Sons 64
Talbot, George 32, 34
Tank Stream 10, 12
Tar-Ra 9, 10
Taylor, Allen (Lord Mayor) 82
Teasel, Harry ('Snowy') **111**
Tench, Watkin 12
theatres 42, 43, 129, 133, 136–7
Thermopylae 49
Thompson, Katherine 137
Thornton, George 25
Towns Place **93**, 135
Towns, Robert **26**, 26–8, 31, 34, 46, 48–50, 55–6, 62
Towns's Wharf 27, 31, 37, 41–2, 49, 52, 57, 69, 100
Towns's Bond Store 64
Townsend, James 21

trade 21, 23–8, 46, 48–50, 54, 62, 77, 93–6, 128
tradesmen 32, 36, 41, 51, 54, 56, 88
Tucker, James 20

U
Underwood, James 19
Underwood, Joseph 16
UNESCO World Heritage Register 127, 129, 132
unionism (*see also* labour movement) 64–7, 98–103
Unsworth Government 122
Unwin, F.W. 23, 33
Unwin St. 30, 36, 55–7, 67, 73
Upper Fort St. 36–7

V
Verge, John 29
Victoria Arms **41**, 90
Victoria Terrace (*see also* Dalgety Terrace) 27, 31, 34, 36–7, 52
'Vinegar Lane' 100

W
Walker, William 21, 24, 25, 55–6
Walker's Wharf 57
Walker Bros & Co. 21, 49–50
Walsh Bay 9, **18**, 20, 21, 24, 25, 29, 32, 49, 55–6, 60, 69, 91, **91**, **94**, 95–6, 119, 121, **124**, 128–9, 134–8
War-Ran 10
warehouses and bond stores 20, 28, 31, 36, 50, 52, 55–7, 69, 90, 97, 116
water supply 33, 51, 99, 109, 137
Waterside Workers Federation 98, 109–10, **109**
Watson Rd. **8**
Watts, Lt. John 40
Wells, William 42
Wentworth, Sophia 27
Wentworth, W.C. 27, 43
Wentworth St. 30, 36, 56–7, 67
West, Josiah 32
Whalers Arms 41
Whaling, whalers 7, 14, 21, 23–6, 28, 37, 46, 49
wharves 19–21, 24–8, 32–2, 34, 36–7, **44**, 48–9, 55–8, 69, 73, 90, 119, **120**, 121, 134
White, Norm 107
Williams, Ann 104
windmills 7, 9, 15, **16**, 17, **19**, **22**
Windmill St. 9, 17, 19, 20, 21, 23, 31–3, 36, 41–2, 46, 53–7, 59, 61–2, 69, 73, **83**, 86, **91**, 91, 112–3, 122
Winsbury Terrace 55
Wolf 25
Wollstonecraft, Edward 21, 24, 25
wool trade 7, 14, 21, 23–26, 28, 32, 37, 46, 49–50, 55–7, **59**, 62–4
Woolloomooloo 96, 101, 118
World War I 89, 93–6, 104, 106
World War II 95, 98, 102, 106, 108–9, 113
Wran Government 119
Wright, James 21

Y
Yates, Theodosia 42
Young Princess Inn 41